I am not assuming that any of my readers
will be accomplished cooks, or even confident ones.
Rather, I am hoping that this little manual
may serve as a gentle guide into what many may suspect
as the unknown, the somewhat frightening area of
creating something out of a bag of groceries,
with only a sprinkling (or less) of knowledge of the stages
involved in getting a meal, or even a dish, on to the table.
Once this has been attempted and the results have been
relatively well received (and no one has died!),
then I hope that the reader will delve deeper and deeper
into the pages and, who knows, perhaps surprise
even themselves, along with their friends.

First
Put on
Your
Apron

Sally
Clarke

2021

Dedicated to the memory of my darling Dads,
Brian Trent Clarke
1926–2004
and to my mother, Sheila, gloriously in her 93rd year...
and, of course, to Samuel

Spring 2021

Sally Clarke Limited
124 Kensington Church Street
London W8 4BH

www.sallyclarke.com

First published in Great Britain by Sally Clarke Limited 2021

ISBN 978-1-5272-9101-0

A CIP catalogue record for this book is available from the British Library.

Printed on Fedrigoni Arena Natural paper
chlorine free, acid free, FSC® mix, heavy metal absence
Typeset in Sabon
Printed and bound in the UK by Gomer Press

Photographer: Lizzie Mayson
Props Stylist: Tabitha Hawkins
Food Stylist: Rosie Ramsden
Food Stylist's Assistant: Rosie French
Designer: Patrick Budge
Editor: Kay Halsey

Contents

Introduction 8

Breakfast... lightish 30

Breakfast... full 54

Lunch... on the run 72

Lunch... no time restrictions 94

Mid-afternoon break... high tea 120

Supper... to fill a gap 142

Supper... to last until breakfast 166

Dinner alone 190

Dinner with everyone 206

Dinner to impress 226

The festive season 250

Index 267

Acknowledgements 271

Introduction

In my kitchen at home I have a very small blue-and-white linen apron, which hangs on the dresser and has done – in the same place – for well over 15 years. It was given to Samuel, our son, when he was a toddler by a kind French friend who lives by the sea in Brittany. We used to wear our (probably matching) aprons together as we podded peas or made pizza dough in those early, precious years. Then, when he eventually grew out of it – and out of being a willing partner at the chopping board – it was washed and ironed and hung in the same spot I find it now.

As he grew older, Samuel's willingness to help in the kitchen was perhaps not as 'automatic' as I would have liked. One reads so often of parents and their offspring piling into the preparation of lunch or supper together and of the healthy discussion and learning that ensues. Sadly, that was not often the case with us. By the time Samuel was into double figures, he had found other distractions, such as homework or violin practice (I wish), which conveniently excused him from being any real help as I prepared the meals.

He nevertheless was, from an early age, a keen and precise critic, and still is. He knows instinctively if I have overcooked the pasta by 30 seconds or under-salted the salad; if I have cut open the homemade English muffins instead of ripping them freshly by hand; or if I have bought the 'wrong' bacon by mistake, which does not crisp so well in the pan, or squeezed oranges for breakfast that are 'not as good as the ones we had in the winter'.

By the age of 17, however, as I started to write this book, his tastes were broadening, becoming more confident in trying new dishes and ingredients on different menus.

Certain elements of his likes and dislikes from the early years remain, such as an aversion to the fat on meat or the keenness to have extra, extra sauce with chicken, beef or duck dishes. His liking of 'anything green' as a child was, I realise now, an absolute blessing. While other children would push away the sprouting broccoli, cabbage and salad leaves, Samuel would relish them and still does – along with 'neat' lemon wedges, fruits of all kinds, olives, spicy saucisson and cured hams, nuts and herbs. Most things sweet or dessert-y have, to date, not been particularly to his taste – except of course for the most extreme varieties of Ben & Jerry's ice creams.

But throughout all this, I am convinced that what helped in his 'edible education' – or even triggered it – were our summer trips to France and Italy from when he was very young. There we would usually plan our days and menus around the farmers' markets and what they had to offer. Samuel would often be part of the troupe of family and friends as we made our daily rounds of the stalls, joining in with the discussions as to which fig looked better than another, or which colour or size of tomato to buy.

Once back at the house, however, the interest somewhat waned, until of course lunch was on the table. The swimming pool or the village tennis court were more of a pull than the kitchen in those days.

At his wonderful school, thoughtful, seasonally inspired menus were put on the table at regular intervals and in copious quantities. At home, meals were put on the table when we were hungry – and tended to be dishes that were prepared and assembled quickly, using short cooking times, often with ingredients from the Restaurant or Shop. In those days, I often served meals on one platter – the meat or fish next to steamed rice or crisp potatoes with a selection of vegetables to one side. This made serving straightforward and portioning easier too, as at one glance I could see how best to divide among the plates. Although I love leftovers (and some dishes can be even better served the day after), at home I still try hard to cook for just that one meal, thereby not creating more than is needed and making each menu different from the last. In our household, one never knew if, at the drop of a hat, we had to be out and about, either with tickets for something or a last-minute booking at a friend's restaurant.

From these tender shoots, Samuel has blossomed into an interested, keen and inventive cook, gleaning as much as he can from the internet of course, but also not afraid to try. He makes the occasional mistakes, as we all do, but learns and grows from them. His interest in 'gadgets' has certainly overtaken mine – but what warmed my heart beyond measure during the lockdown Christmas was seeing the joy on his face when he unwrapped a recently re-lined copper pan, which I bought at Dehillerin in Paris when I was studying there, aged 21. Over the years it had become badly scratched and beyond being safe to use, but now the pan is almost pristine once more and destined to become a treasured part of his future kitchen, wherever that will end up being, once university life is behind him.

My original thoughts and aspirations for this book were varied, centred around the wish that young people, about to leave home, school or college as Samuel once did, would be able to look after themselves wholesomely (and with a degree of confidence and joy) without having to resort to the convenience foods or the quick, cheap and easy alternatives that are too often found within reach of the doorsteps of our universities. I remember well being fearful for his sustenance, wellbeing and general health during his years away from my watchful eye and that of his school, as he moved from the safe lifeline of meals on the table at fixed times and a relatively well-stocked fridge.

I am sure that this anxiety is mirrored in each and every household up and down the land, as families near the time for their young to start fending for themselves.

However, due to a busy life at the Restaurant, plus the juggling of various 2020 lockdowns and a constantly changing tier system within the hospitality industry, the timing of this book has perhaps rather missed the boat for Samuel, now that he is about to complete his finals.

But there will be other young people out there and indeed I am hoping that the following chapters will also be useful and comforting to others who, for various reasons have, until now, rarely ventured towards a kitchen, let alone into an oven. Young adults who have perhaps focused more on building their career, having to sustain themselves along the way on bought-in ready meals, grabbing snacks along the way, never having the time or interest to create a meal for themselves. Or they may have simply dined out every night if their salaries have allowed.

Then there is the generation who have gone through life supported by a spouse or partner in all things culinary, having never needed to raise a finger other than the occasional washing-up duties, and now find themselves alone, perhaps for the first time, and who are at a complete loss as to where to start.

In these days of endless searching for a perfect work-life balance that includes 'downtime' and stress-relieving activities, cooking can be therapeutic and calming – a way to slow down the pace of life as well as to acquire new skills. The emergence of home delivery helps, too; with one quick click, the staple kitchen ingredients may be planned for and bought in advance, allowing a more relaxed time to shop for the special items in a market closer to the time of cooking.

I would love to think that this book would be a guide and a helping hand for many – and perhaps even a crutch to some – as nothing within is complicated. I have tried to explain each step along the way simply, yet thoroughly, enough to give the reader confidence, and ultimately the energy, to take each recipe through to its natural conclusion – and to the finished dish that can be presented and served with pride.

Each recipe is marked with a *, ** or *** in the index, denoting its simplicity (or relative complexity) to prepare and cook.

Each section is divided into Spring and Summer, and Autumn and Winter and therefore acts as a gentle indicator to the reader as to which ingredients may be suitable and available at the time. As customers of the Restaurant and Shops or readers of my last books will know only too well, this is of course so important to me as a cook.

Creating dishes that are appropriate to the season, the weather or the occasion is vital and I cannot emphasise this point fiercely enough. Asparagus in November, raspberries in January or pumpkin in June are simply not right – they don't feel right, taste right or look right – put simply, they are NOT right.

So, I recommend that you try, whenever it is possible or practicable, not to plan your menu or dish until you have chosen your ingredients. Of course, have an idea of what ideally you would like to prepare beforehand but let the season guide you, along with the available fruits, vegetables and herbs around you, and let your instinct take you to the combination of flavours and textures that will suit the occasion.

Allow the following pages to help you find not only confidence at your chopping board but eventually a steady path to the creation of a taste and style that you can call your own. But first – put on that apron!

The kitchen cupboard

Which kitchen could operate without salt, pepper and olive oil? If there is room for nothing else in the 'dry store', space must be made for these: ideally a flaky sea salt, a mixture of white and black peppercorns in a pepper grinder and a good olive oil. The oil need not be an extravagant one, but it should have a pleasing flavour with which to dress salads and vegetables. A less expensive vegetable oil, such as rapeseed or sunflower, can serve as the base cooking oil for vegetables, fish, meats and poultry.

A selection of dry ingredients, such as delicious, nutritious and often inexpensive grains, rice and pulses, from lentils and beans to split peas, along with dried fruits, nuts and spices, forms a good basis for many a tasty dish. Of course, pasta of all kinds is known and loved almost the world over, and no kitchen cupboard should be without it. The dried varieties will last (seemingly) forever and a selection of shapes and sizes can be chosen to have on hand for emergencies, and for the occasions when a quick and very simple meal is needed. And don't forget rolled oats for breakfast porridge and muesli; a small bag (unless lots of baking is going to be done) of plain flour; and sugar, if needed, for tea and coffee.

Gone are the days when to be a vegetarian was problematic – at the very least frowned upon or, at its worst, something of which to be scared. Many more people are comfortable now preparing food for those who prefer not to eat meat or fish. In fact, the days of shock and horror at finding a main course 'sans' meat placed in front of us are rapidly disappearing. Even those who normally love to include hunks of protein in their daily menu could, dare I say should, from time to time eschew meat or fish throughout the week, if the kitchen has even a few of these staple dry stores at hand.

Not only saving on expense, vegetarian menus are also relatively straightforward to prepare and cook, and at the same time offer a varied diet of dishes, from nourishing, spicy chickpea, vegetable and herb broths in the winter months to refreshing fruit and vegetable salads in the summer, tossed with grains, nuts and herbs.

The fridge and freezer

I am convinced that one reason the 'use by' and 'best before' dates on our perishable food labels are so draconian is that many a household fridge cannot be trusted to maintain a consistent temperature of 3–5°C. Added to this, the rubber door seals are often past their own 'best before' date, and therefore the fresh food stored within does not stand a chance of surviving for long.

In rented student accommodation, fridges and ovens are often not regarded by landlords as equipment worth extravagance, so my advice would be to inspect these well before signing an agreement and make sure that they are put into good working order, or even replaced, before the move.

As soon as you move in, defrost the freezer compartment, and make fresh ice cubes. Old ice can harbour smells and tastes – and who wants old ice cubes in their drink, anyway? Give the fridge a good clean both inside and out with warm, soapy water. Remove the shelves and salad drawers, too, and wash and rinse them well, as one never knows what has been lurking in there over the past year.

The oven and hob

These should undergo an equally thorough check. Make sure that the hob works efficiently and that the grill or salamander is in good working order. Ovens are more difficult to clean than fridges, and will take more elbow grease. Nevertheless, 30 minutes on this will be time well spent, using an abrasive cleaner to get all of last year's fat and grime wiped away. Inside the oven, you will need to use oven cleaner without a doubt, unless you have luckily chanced on a brand new one. A pair of rubber gloves should not be sniffed at here – use them with pride!

While you are in the cleaning mode, do the shelves and cupboards as well, throwing anything away that looks suspect, and then finally wash and clean the floor. I promise, you will feel much better when this is all done.

Shopping rules

A farmers' market is my aspirational key to a great menu, as it is here that one can interact with and support small businesses and growers. And – especially helpful for the budget-conscious among us – one is able to buy single items and to pick and choose what looks good on the day, thus creating the perfect balance of seasonal ingredients, from the farm to the plate.

However, not every city or town is blessed with a farmers' market. Instead, perhaps there is a street market or farm shop near to you that sells locally produced items. Failing this, although a supermarket will offer everything from pineapples to pumpkins and from cabbages to coriander, no matter what the season, if you browse the chilled cabinets and shelves you will find that, in essence, the less expensive items are the ones that a) have travelled the shortest distance and b) are in plentiful supply – i.e. in season! While some supermarkets now buy from farms in their locality, not all do. And there is still an alarming number that even sell apples from the southern hemisphere in the autumn, when of course our British orchards are overflowing.

Even if you are not sure of what vegetable, salad, herb or fruit to choose, the look of the item will tell you. It will be crisper, fresher, brighter and simply more appealing than something that may have been picked a week or two before, and transported by air, sea, road or rail, across miles and miles... and we don't want that, do we?

Think of the ideal: to pick or dig something from your own back yard. Failing this, what is the closest to that? A friend who grows their own, a farmer on the outskirts of town, a farm shop, pick-your-own farm or a street market will often provide the best quality at affordable prices.

If all else fails, you will have to choose the best supermarket or provisions shop in your area. This may not be easy, as it will often come down to convenience and which one will save you the most time and money. Which one has the best rotation of stock? You need to see a fresh display each time you visit the shop – not just the same vegetables rearranged day after day. A popular, busy shop or supermarket will rotate its stock all the time, fresh supplies will be delivered often, and therefore the ingredients on show will often be the best they have. A shop that is not busy will not have such a steady rotation of goods and, while the pricing may be appealing, the quality may not be so.

Experience will show you in time that, while a freshly picked cabbage may cost a little more, it will last a lot longer in your fridge and will be packed with more nutrients. Far better to choose this rather than the tired, less expensive one that has been sitting on a dusty shelf for a few days.

Buy fresh ingredients in small quantities, often. Whenever possible, buy them on instinct, not from a list. Make lists for the store-cupboard and household items.

On returning home, unpack the shopping immediately. In the fridge, place the newer items at the back, so that the older ingredients are more visible and will therefore be used first.

The same principle should apply to the store-cupboard items – even though the 'use by' or 'best before' dates will be longer, a system of rotation is good practice here, too.

Kitchen rules

Wash your hands

Wear an apron

Keep it simple

Remember that the prep work is key

Make a task list before starting

Clear up as you go

Don't drink (too much) until the food is on the table

Do not leave knives in the sink

Wipe down the surfaces often

Lay the table – as if setting a stage

Give everyone a napkin (kitchen roll will do)

Equipment

While good-quality kitchen kit is expensive, there are a few basics that you will need to create even the simplest of dishes. However, not everyone has the funds for high-end equipment and, especially in rented student accommodation, some may be at the mercy of a landlord with slightly different priorities.

Work your way steadily down this list, seeing the top few items as essential, then perhaps borrowing some pieces from family and gradually, as funds permit, adding the slightly less necessary items later.

Chopping board

Knives:

  small paring

  serrated

  long and heavy for chopping

Steel for sharpening – ask someone to teach you how

3–4 pans of various depths and sizes – ideally heavy-based

Wooden spoons

Peeler

Grater

Palette knife or spatula

Electric kettle

Toaster

Tongs

Large sieve for draining pasta and vegetables

Juicer – electric or manual

Tea towels – to be washed as often as your pants

Oven gloves

Rubber gloves

Liquidiser or food processsor

Menu planning – planning ahead

Some, or perhaps I should say most, of the recipes in this book are perfect for preparing, cooking and serving on the same day. Others will fare well, or even better, if made in advance. Some may be made in stages, such as the rabbit with pappardelle, which allows the fiddly, time-consuming work to be done on Day 1 and the rest to assemble and serve the following day. Others, particularly of the baked or dessert variety, may be kept on hand for a rainy day – for when friends or (heaven forbid!) family drop in unexpectedly, such as the shortbread biscuits, tea bread and apricot-vanilla jam. Remember, that for many a dish, there are 'run-offs': A roasted chicken one day may become an open chicken sandwich with mozzarella and basil the next, or a delicious warming, nourishing chicken broth or risotto the day after.

There is a lot to be said for doing a little preparation and planning of the menu before embarking on a dish or two. Map out in your mind how you see the 'flow' of the meal. Will there be a starter or just a main course? Should the starter be prepared in advance and ready to serve, thus allowing time to focus on the intricacies of the main course? Will there be a dessert that needs cooking while you are all eating? Or will you serve a simple bowl of fresh fruit, such as clementines, cherries, apricots or grapes, instead? Or a cold dessert left chilling in the fridge?

Consider if you are the sort of cook who needs peace and quiet in order to concentrate on your preparation, or if you revel in friends piling into the kitchen to help with vegetable peeling and washing up, merrily sampling the wines as they go.

Personally, I am firmly rooted in the former camp and can think of nothing worse than guests arriving 30 minutes earlier than planned, but we are all different.

Whichever style makes you feel confident in your kitchen, plan some time to lay the table – even if it is simply a pile of plates and cutlery at one end and glasses and bottles at the other. Do you want candles, flowers, lights on or off, windows wide open or tight shut? What mood do you want to give the occasion – or do you prefer just to let it happen? But at least give it some thought.

One golden rule for me has always been to do as much of the washing up and clearing up as is humanly possible before sitting down to eat. If you follow this advice, you will not only have the maximum crockery, cutlery and glasses at your disposal, but there will also be ample room for all the dirties once the table is cleared. A clear sink is a dream. The second golden rule is to always have a boiling kettle at the ready. You can never underestimate the number of things that need hot water in a hurry: pasta, fresh vegetables, loosening up a sauce, warming a sauce jug or simply for coffee or tea.

I am not assuming that any of my readers will be accomplished cooks, or even confident ones. Rather, I am hoping that this little manual may serve as a gentle guide into what many may suspect as the unknown, the somewhat frightening area of creating something out of a bag of groceries, with only a sprinkling (or less) of knowledge of the stages involved in getting a meal, or even a dish, on to the table. Once this has been attempted and the results have been relatively well received (and no one has died!), then I hope that the reader will delve deeper and deeper into the pages and, who knows, perhaps surprise even themselves, along with their friends.

Some of my most special moments during my young life at college in Paris were spent shopping, cooking and eating with my fellow students. Each weekend we would search out the best street markets, writing our menus along the way, as we chose the ingredients. Then, at a different friend's apartment each time, we would spend the rest of the day preparing and cooking, which would culminate in us all being seated together around a beautiful, long candlelit table for a huge dinner of many courses.

While I have a romantic view that this slice of life should, at some stage, be part of everyone's education, I have no doubt that the academic pressure on today's students, compared to my own experience over 30 years ago, makes this much more difficult. I would, nevertheless, love to believe that each student could, from time to time, find a slot in their busy schedule to visit a farmers' market or a street stall and to create, if not a meal, just a dish, and if not a dish, to enjoy one piece of fruit or a vegetable. This would be instead of taking the shortest possible route to satisfying their hunger, which is, more often than not, the cheapest, quickest and the least wholesome of all options.

A few tips and strict rules

How to wash up

I remember my first O Level cookery lesson in the early Sixties with Mrs Potts – not a joke! – a tall, well-built lady of a certain age, from Yorkshire, with a shrill, high-pitched voice that, I discovered decades later, mirrored that of Julia Child. (If you are not familiar with her work, please look her up.) That day, Mrs Potts instructed us all in the art of washing up. Hot soapy water was the key, followed by the order in which the dirty items were to be dealt with. It occurred to me recently, while watching my son (very kindly) washing up, that a few simple guidelines may be helpful to readers of this book.

First, stack the washing up neatly together on one side of the sink, plates having been scraped of debris, and glasses emptied. Pots, pans and roasting tins, usually being the dirtiest of all, should be kept separate from the rest. Some of them may need 'soaking' first, for example a roasting tin or a baking tray that may have bits of food encrusted on the base. Simply leave these on one side, filled with a little warm water, and deal with them later. The other side of the sink should be used for the draining, and in the absence of a draining rack, a clean tea towel or cloth on the work surface will do nicely. (I often use both – one for delicate items, one for more robust items such as plates and bowls.)

If using rubber gloves, put them on now, and collect the cloth or washing-up brush. Run the water into the sink until hot, then place the plug firmly in the hole (or use the washing-up bowl). Add washing-up liquid and turn the tap to run very slowly. As the sink (or bowl) is slowly filling, start by washing the glasses, one by one, carefully lifting them out of the hot soapy water to be rinsed under the gently running water. Place each glass upside down on the draining tea towel. Next, place the cutlery in the soapy water and clean them one by one, again rinsing under the running water. Place them in the draining rack. The plates should be next, placing a small pile in the soapy water at a time, washing them using the cloth or brush, then rinsing under the running water, remembering that the underside of each plate needs to be washed as well as the top.

Once all the tableware is clean, stop the running water and start washing the cooking equipment and utensils, the cleanest first and the dirtiest last. Rinse the items with a little fresh hot water each time, and keep them away from the plates and glasses to keep these more fragile items safe. (I often place them on the cooker top or even in the cooling oven, so that they dry quickly.) Kitchen knives need special attention and should be washed one by one, in the hot soapy water, rinsed, then left away from the other items, for safety.

Using a clean tea towel, dry each item, in the order that they have been washed, so that the delicate items are put away first. Lastly, have a good look around the kitchen for anything that may have been forgotten, wipe down the surfaces with a hot soapy cloth and drain the sink, rinsing it until clean. Check that the draining area is clean and dry also.

How to settle a chopping board

Remember that an onion or piece of garlic will taint a knife and chopping board and therefore they should not be used for the slicing of fruit, for example, without thoroughly washing and drying them first. In an ideal world, you should have two chopping boards in your kitchen, for this very reason, allowing you to keep certain jobs separate. Also, after fish or meat preparation, always scrub the board well, and dry it before using it for the next task, as well as the knife you have used.

As an experiment, try putting a chopping board straight on a table top, place the palm of your hand on this and move the board about. See how easy it is to slide? Now, place a dishcloth or damp tea towel under the board, press down gently and you will find that it will have settled into place. It is now safe to crush garlic, dice onions, slice carrots or chop nuts, without fear of everything flying off into an irretrievable mess on the floor or, even worse, a knife skidding in the wrong direction, resulting in cuts or stitches.

How to dice an onion

Place a damp cloth or tea towel on the table, as above, to settle the chopping board on top, preventing the board from slipping while you are dicing, slicing or chopping. First, trim the top end and any excess root hairs from the onion, then cut exactly in half, through the root to the top. Leaving the half-root firmly attached, peel the outside skin away from the top. This may be one or two layers, depending on the age of the onion, but you need to end up with a fresh-looking peeled onion without any tough skin covering it.

Lay the onion halves on the board cut side down. Using a small-to-medium-sized sharp-pointed knife, cut into the onion with the blade pointing towards the root in several parallel slices vertically down the length of the onion. Do not cut the onion apart, rather allow the knife tip to reach the root but no further.

Next, place your knife blade horizontally with the board and, using the palm of your other hand to press down gently on the top of the onion, slice it in half from the top end to towards the root end, but not reaching the root. In this way, you will have kept the onion intact. Finally, holding the onion together at its sides, while carefully keeping your fingertips out of the way, slice the onion vertically across the width of the onion from the top towards the root. What you should now have on your board is a beautifully diced onion. Practise at first with wide slices of say ½cm each time, then, as you get more practised, you can venture on to the fine dice, which are perfect for the base of a risotto, for example.

How to slice vegetables

The general rule is to start as before. Settle your chopping board with a damp cloth or tea towel. This will prevent the board from slipping, which in turn will prevent your knife and fingers from slipping.

Carrots: wash, peel and trim the ends. If large, cut in half lengthwise then, with the cut surfaces on the board downwards, slice the carrot with a medium-large, heavy, sharp knife. I like to cut on a slight angle rather than straight across, as I think it makes the finished dish look more interesting and attractive. If the carrots are small and you prefer to keep them whole, take care when slicing as their rounded sides will make them slippery. Holding the carrot at the top, start cutting even-width slices from the pointed end towards the top of the carrot, using firm, rhythmic slicing movements.

Courgettes: the same as before, except that I prefer not to peel them first.

Celery: trim away the root end (and the top end if discoloured), and discard. Next, trim away a little more of the root end, which will release the individual sticks. Keep this end, the outer sticks and any dark leaves for stocks and soups once they have been thoroughly washed. Use the more tender sticks inside and the pale green leaves for salads and garnishing cheese plates. Wash well to remove any grit. To dice, cut the sticks into even-sized, manageable lengths. Cut each of these lengthwise into 2, 3 or 4 depending on how fine a dice you want. Then gather the sticks together into small bundles like soldiers. Holding one of these bundles together firmly, slice across with a medium-large, heavy, sharp knife, keeping your fingertips clear of the blade as you work your way up the length of the bundle. Then follow the same procedure with the remaining bundles.

How to blanch and peel tomatoes

Take a pan large enough to hold the tomatoes, half fill with water and bring to the boil. Meanwhile, use a small, sharp knife to make a nick in the skin of each tomato by the stem end. Using a bowl or slotted spoon, lower them into the boiling water carefully, to avoid splashing. Over a high heat, bring the water back to the boil rapidly. After a few seconds, remove one tomato with a slotted spoon and attempt to peel it from the slash mark. If the skin peels away easily, they are ready. If not, leave them in a few seconds longer. Do not overcook the tomatoes or you will soon have a very watery tomato soup!

Turn off the heat and either remove the tomatoes one by one with a slotted spoon or carefully pour the contents of the pan into a colander in the sink. Either way, get cold running water over the tomatoes as soon as possible to halt the cooking. Alternatively, place the blanched tomatoes in a bowl of iced water and leave them to soak for a minute or two. Peel them carefully, keeping the skins for a stock or soup if needed.

How to crush garlic

Place a damp cloth or tea towel on the table, as before, to settle the chopping board on top, preventing the board from slipping while you are working. Break a clove away from the bulb and lay it on the clean chopping board. Press the 'heel' of your biggest knife using the palm of your hand over the top of it, flat side parallel with the board, thus squashing the clove almost flat. The papery skin will have come loose and this can now be easily peeled away and discarded. Remove the green shoot within, if present.

Sprinkle the peeled clove with a pinch or two of salt then, using the flat side of the tip of a medium-sized knife, squash the clove into the board, again and again, until the garlic has become a creamy paste. Scrape this into a small container. Covered with a few drops of olive oil, it will last a day or two in the fridge.

The most important thing to do now is to scrub the board, the knife and your hands well, rinse with hot water and dry. Sniff both the board and the knife carefully and, if any trace of garlic remains, you need to wash them again. There is nothing worse than tasting a perfect piece of fruit, for example, that has been sliced on a tainted chopping board or with a tainted knife. (And it is not just domestic cooks that fall foul of this mistake – the staff of many a 'professional' kitchen has been known to make this criminal error.)

How to chop herbs, such as thyme, rosemary or sage

These herbs make a wonderful difference to a dish, be it vegetable, fish or meat-based. However, eating them whole before cooking is nigh on impossible – one needs to chop them very finely, or to fry, simmer or roast them to make them palatable and digestible.

First, run your index finger and thumb down the stems, one by one, to release the leaves. (Save the stalks for stocks and soups.) Next, with one hand push the leaves together in a bundle on a settled chopping board. While holding them firmly, slice a good, large, sharp knife through them in short intervals, chopping them as finely as you can safely manage.

Once this is done, try chopping them by holding the point of the knife firmly downwards on the board and rapidly moving the handle of the knife up and down across the herbs, thus chopping them finer and finer as you go. The sharper the knife, the finer you will be able to chop, and the more dangerous this exercise will be. As with most things, practice will make perfect.

How to chop soft herbs: parsley, chervil or tarragon

Wash the herbs gently and, holding the stalks together, flick the excess water off before running your index finger and thumb down the stems to release the leaves. (Save the stalks for stocks and soups). With one hand, push the leaves together into a bundle on a settled chopping board. While holding them firmly, slice a good, large, sharp knife through them at short intervals, chopping them as finely as you can safely manage. For most soft herbs, this will be sufficient, as they tend to be delicious just as they are. However, if a quick extra chop is required to create a more even size, cut across the herbs as described above until you have reached the desired finish.

How to chop chives

Remove any discoloured or damaged shoots and trim the dry ends. Gather the chives together in a straight, parallel bundle and hold them together with one hand. Using a sharp knife, slice from the root end upwards towards the tips in short, fine slices or, if you prefer longer 'batons', slice them at 1cm intervals.

How to slice spring onions

From each onion, remove the outer leaf, which may be discoloured or bruised. Trim the root ends and the tips carefully. Wash gently under a cold running tap and shake dry. Gather the bunch back together tightly with one hand and place on the chopping board. Using a sharp knife, slice across from the tips towards the root, as finely or wide as you wish. I prefer to keep the white separate from the green, but most recipes use both parts together.

Food safety

Washing your hands constantly during food preparation is good practice; coughing or sneezing over the food, or into your hands, certainly is not. Your wellbeing and that of your guests should be at the front of your mind when preparing and cooking food.

Buying fresh ingredients from trusted sources certainly makes a good start to this process, but once you get them to your kitchen, they need care at every step of the way towards the plate or the lunchbox.

Your nose, eyes and taste buds will be the best guide of all. If you taste something and it does not seem quite right, your instincts are telling you that this should probably be avoided.

A little mouldy fur on the surface of a pot of jam can easily be scooped away and the jam beneath will remain perfectly fit for eating. However, if mouldy fur is found on a leftover chicken or beef stew, this should be discarded. A waste, I know, but better that than giving your friends food poisoning and the probability of being off work for 3 days to recover.

If a leftover soup or sauce is found bubbling (fermenting) in the fridge, showing slow bubbles rising to the surface, it is a sign that it has turned sour and needs to be thrown out.

Hard cheeses, by their very nature, are liable to attract mould on the cut surfaces over time, but these may simply be trimmed away to reveal the perfectly good cheese inside. Soft cheeses have a shorter shelf life and the instructions on the packaging regarding best-before dates should be noted and adhered to.

Storage

Not everything needs fridge space. Some ingredients, such as slightly unripe fruit, potatoes and bananas, are better off stored in a cool, not cold place. However, make sure that meat, fish, shellfish, dairy, salads, soft cheeses and soft fruits are stored in the fridge. They should be wrapped or covered to prevent contamination, and anything likely to leak (such as raw meat or fish) should be laid on a dish and then covered, to prevent dripping onto other items.

Never put anything warm or hot into a fridge as this will raise the temperature inside and put other ingredients at risk. Keep unprepared ingredients, such as vegetables or fruit straight from the market or shop, separate from ingredients that have been washed and prepared. Equally, keep cooked dishes separate from raw foods. If it is likely that you are going to keep cooked ingredients or dishes for more than a day, it is advisable to label the container with the date you made it, and possibly noting the name of the dish also. After all, a puréed leek and potato soup can look very like a gooseberry fool after a day or two.

Always check the use-by date on bought-in prepared foods, meat, fish, cream and soft cheeses. A good rule of thumb is that dishes including cooked meat or fish will last 3 days if kept cool in a fridge at 3–5°C. In other words, if you cook it on a Monday, it will be good to eat until last thing on Wednesday. Cooked vegetarian items, including grains, vegetables, cheese, eggs, cream or milk, will last well for up to 5 days in a fridge of the same temperature.

When reheating leftovers, cook them thoroughly, making sure that the heat penetrates all the way to the centre. One of the most dangerous things you can do during food preparation is to half-cook an item that has been cooked once before, by just warming the dish. In some extreme cases, this can risk the chance of bacterial growth within, which could lead to very unpleasant consequences – sickness and diarrhoea at the very least.

So, on that happy note, good luck to you all – and let's get going!

Recipe ratings

These ratings signify the level of confidence required to accomplish a more than acceptable dish. You can find them with each recipe in the index on page 267.

*   TECHNICALLY STRAIGHTFORWARD
**   REQUIRING BASIC TECHNIQUE
***   REQUIRING TIME AND MODEST TECHNIQUE

Breakfast... lightish

While the easiest and quickest way to ease
a hungry stomach in the morning may well be a carton of juice and
a slice or two of bread – toasted, buttered and spread with jam or
marmalade – they do not raise the spirits and give a spring to the step
in quite the same way as the following ideas, which could make
the start of the day that little bit special.

Spring and Summer

Pink grapefruit and blood orange segments
Yogurt, blueberry and strawberry smoothie
Granola with oats, apricot, dates and almonds
Seeded granary bread
Apricot and vanilla jam

Autumn and Winter

Winter fruit salad and mixed winter juices
Bircher muesli with nuts and apple
Warm porridge with brown sugar
Hot mocha drink with whipped cream

Pink grapefruit & blood orange segments

1 PINK GRAPEFRUIT AND 1 LARGE BLOOD ORANGE PER PERSON

Segment the fruits: first, cut off the top and bottom of each using a small to medium sharp knife, just enough to expose the pink or orange flesh beneath. With one flat surface firmly on the chopping board – see page 22 for settling the board – slice 'petals' of peel away from the fruits, carefully keeping the knife just between the pith and the juicy fruit.

Next, holding the fruits one by one over a bowl, cut the segments away from the dividing membrane, by sliding the knife between each segment. Finally, squeeze the remaining clump of membrane to extract as much extra juice as possible, then discard. Leave the juicy segments of the fruits in the fridge in a small serving dish, covered until ready to serve.

Yogurt, blueberry & strawberry smoothie

Throughout the year, you can chop and change the fruits to suit the season and your taste. Try raspberries, blackberries, peaches, nectarines or apricots, for example. The banana is good to use throughout the year, however, as it not only stabilises the purée, but also brings 'bulk' to the finished drink as well.

MAKES 2–4 GLASSES, DEPENDING ON SIZE
2 ripe bananas, peeled
1 punnet (approximately 125g) blueberries
1 punnet (approximately 200g) strawberries, green leaf removed
400ml whole milk
100g plain yogurt
A few ice cubes
A little honey or sugar, to taste (optional)

Place the bananas, blueberries and strawberries in a liquidiser with the milk, yogurt, ice cubes and honey or sugar (if required). Purée until smooth and bright pink, then pour into a jug. Drink as soon as you can.

Alternatively, if you do not have access to a liquidiser, place the fruit in a bowl and mash with a fork until very runny. Add the liquid ingredients little by little, whisking with a fork or whisk. Taste, then pour over the ice cubes. This method will result in a slightly chunky texture, but it will still be delicious, and may be eaten with a spoon instead of drinking it straight.

For a dairy-free version, replace the milk and yogurt with cranberry or apple juice. Purée as above and serve as soon as possible, as the smoothie will separate within a few minutes.

Granola with oats, apricot, dates & almonds

Often, when I return home late after a long day at the Restaurant, and having not had time to eat much, I will satisfy my hunger with a bowl of yogurt, sliced fresh fruit and a sprinkling of granola. I then sleep like a baby.

At our Bakery, we have made the same granola recipe for over 25 years, and continue to use the same methods of mixing, toasting, stirring and cooling as we always have. The list of seeds, nuts, grains and fruits also remains unchanged, and we sell huge amounts of granola throughout the year, not only in the Shops but also to our many wholesale customers at the Bakery.

That recipe will remain a secret! However, the ingredients listed and the method that follows are both similar, and will create a pleasing, tasty and wholesome breakfast (or midnight snack) to add to your repertoire.

Made in a large batch, it will last for up to 3 weeks if kept in a cool place in an airtight container. You could also bag it up with a pretty ribbon or raffia to give as an unusual gift, perhaps for a birthday, anniversary or other celebration.

The balance and variety of ingredients may be altered to your own individual taste, but keep to the approximate weights and volumes as closely as possible.

Serve with plain or fruit yogurt and fresh fruit of your choice. »

MAKES ENOUGH FOR 20–25 PORTIONS
(DEPENDING ON YOUR APPETITE/GREED!)
200g honey or maple syrup, or half and half
4tbsp sunflower, coconut, peanut or olive oil, or a mixture
Generous pinch cinnamon
Generous pinch sea salt
200g rolled oats
100g flaked barley, rye or spelt
60g almonds, skins on or off, roughly chopped
45g hazelnuts, roughly chopped
60g pumpkin and sunflower seeds, mixed
30g dried apricots, sliced
50g raisins or sultanas, separated if stuck together
20g dates, chopped

Heat the oven to 150°C/fan oven 130°C/mark 2.

Warm the honey, syrup, oil, cinnamon and sea salt together over a low heat in a small pan until just warm and liquid.

Mix the oats, barley, nuts and seeds together in a bowl. Pour the warm liquid in and stir until everything is well coated.

Line a baking sheet with greaseproof or silicone paper and spread the mixture over evenly. Bake in the oven for 20 minutes, then remove from the oven and stir gently, so that the parts around the edges are moved into the middle and vice versa. This will make sure the granola bakes evenly.

Continue to bake for a further 10–15 minutes, then remove from the oven and allow to cool, while stirring occasionally to break up any large clumps. Add the dried fruits and stir well together.

Stored in an airtight container, the granola will last up to 3 weeks, but is best eaten as fresh as possible.

Seeded granary bread

At our Bakery we make all our breads using a levain, a sour dough starter. This not only lengthens the inherently slow production time, but it also increases the depth of flavour within the dough, assists the beautifully aerated texture and prolongs the keeping quality. This recipe uses commercial yeast which is readily available in most shops, and is quick and easy to use. It produces a slightly more dense, robust texture, but the addition of grains and seeds makes it a pleasingly more-ish loaf, suitable for breakfast and tea time.

MAKES 1 LARGE LOAF

400g mixed flours, ideally malted grain bread flour, wholemeal flour or
  granary bread flour
100g white bread flour, plus a little for sprinkling
1½tsp fine salt
20g mixed seeds, such as sunflower, pumpkin, sesame or linseed
300ml warm water
1tsp honey
1tbsp olive oil
7g dried yeast or 10g fresh yeast

Place the flours, salt and the seeds in a bowl. In another bowl, mix the water, honey, olive oil and yeast until smooth. Pour the liquid into the dry ingredients and stir together with a wooden spoon – or (literally) by hand, which I prefer – until everything is combined.

Remove the dough from the bowl and place on a clean table top or chopping board, and knead until it is smooth and springy to the touch. If it feels dry, add a little extra water, or if it feels too sticky, add a little extra flour. (A golden rule that should not be ignored, which I was taught 100 years ago at baking college – and have never forgotten – is 'the wetter the dough, the better the dough'.) »

Kneading is a method that involves stretching the dough as it is turned over and around. This will take 5–10 minutes and may feel like hard work, but the result of this labour will be such a treat once the loaf comes out of the oven. The internet is a great place to see bread being kneaded, so get a few tips before you start. I recommend Richard Bertinet – thebertinetkitchen.com, Dan Lepard – danlepard.com or bbcgoodfood.com for guidance.

Place the dough back in the bowl, cover with clingfilm and allow to rise (expand in size by half again) for up to 60 minutes in a warm place. Remove from the bowl and gently shape the loaf into a round or long shape and place on a baking sheet, lined with a sheet of baking parchment'. Cover again and allow to rise as before for 30–40 minutes. Meanwhile, heat the oven to 200°C/fan oven 180°C/mark 6.

Sprinkle the loaf with a little extra flour and bake for 15–20 minutes, then reduce the temperature to 180°C/fan oven 160°C/mark 4 and continue to bake until the crust is well formed and golden brown, approximately 20–30 more minutes. The loaf should sound hollow when tapped on the underside. Allow to cool on a wire rack before slicing.

If individual rolls are preferred, shape the dough into 6–10 equal-sized balls and place, well spaced, on the baking sheet. Cover and allow to rise for 30 minutes, then bake on the middle shelf, as above, for 10–15 minutes. Turn the oven down to 180°C/fan oven 160°C/mark 4 and continue to bake for 5–10 minutes or until the rolls are golden brown and sound hollow when tapped underneath.

Apricot & vanilla jam

Buy more apricots than you think you need and make sure they are ripe and luscious-looking – as this is the only way to make luscious-tasting jam.

MAKES 3 X 500G JARS
2kg ripe apricots (or peaches or nectarines – or a mixture of all, depending on the season)
1.4kg granulated sugar
½ vanilla pod or 1tsp vanilla essence
2 small lemons, juice

When you get the fruit home, scrub the biggest, heaviest stainless-steel pan you have, until it is sparkling clean. Trim away any badly bruised or discoloured parts of the fruit. Pull each apricot in half at the crease and discard the kernel, then cut each half roughly into 2. (Cut the flesh away from the peaches or nectarines using a small knife, discarding the stones.) Do this while holding the fruits over the pan so that you do not lose even one drop of the precious juice. Pour the sugar over and gently stir together, adding the vanilla pod, if using. Cover and leave in a cool place for 1–2 hours or preferably overnight. This will allow the fruits to 'macerate' and will help to pull out the juices.

Assuming that you are able to be attentive for up to 1 hour, place the pan over a low heat. As the mixture starts to bubble around the edges, give it a gentle stir, but try hard not to get sugar up the sides of the pan (you chemists will understand why...). If you are not able to be attentive, leave it until you are, as this needs focus!

Allow the mixture to bubble at a gentle boil, stirring occasionally but not too often, to make sure it is not sticking to the bottom of the pan. After 20-25 minutes, the jam will have reduced and will need testing for 'the set'. »

Take the pan off the heat and, using a teaspoon, place a little of the juice on to a saucer or plate. Put this into the fridge. If, after 3–4 minutes, the jam seems to have softly set, your jam is nearly ready. Hooray! (If you are a scientist and have a clean thermometer handy, you can skip this step – the mixture needs to reach 104°C.)

If, on the other hand, it seems a little too liquid, return it to the heat and continue to cook as before for a few extra minutes, then test again. I always aim for a 'soft-set', which retains the brightness of colour as well as a more pleasing texture. Jams that are cooked for too long tend to be lacklustre in colour and often difficult to 'scoop' once set.

Now, put the pan back on the heat and add the lemon juice and the vanilla essence (if not using the vanilla pod). Bring back to a rolling boil for only a minute, then remove from the heat.

Meanwhile, you need to prepare the jam jars or pots in which you are planning to store the jam. These can be old or new, used or pristine – they simply need to be without chips or cracks, and with lids that fit perfectly.

Heat the oven to 130°C/fan oven 110°C/mark 1. Wash and rinse the jam jars well, then place them carefully on a baking sheet. Heat the jars in the oven for 10 minutes, then turn the oven off, leaving the jars safely in the oven until you are ready to fill them. Next, place the jam jar lids in a small pan and cover with hot water. Bring to the boil for 1–2 minutes, then drain the pan.

You are now ready to pot the jam. Remove the hot jars from the oven. Using a scrupulously clean spoon or ladle, scoop the jam into the jars up to their necks. Using oven gloves or tongs, place the hot lids on the jars and screw tightly shut. Phew! You've made it – well done!

When they have cooled down, wash and dry the jars very well, making sure that the lids are firmly screwed on. Store them in a cool, dark place for up to 4 months, but once a jar has been opened, keep it in the fridge and eat within 2 weeks (not difficult, I can assure you). Don't forget to save one jar of jam to give away to that special friend!

Winter fruit salad

SERVES 1–2
1 large orange
1 red- or pink-skinned apple
1 ripe pear
A few raisins
2 dates
3 dried apricots, sliced

Slice the top and bottom from the orange and, with one cut surface face down on the chopping board, cut away the 'petals' of the peel, so that no pith remains. Practice will perfect this art (see page 32).

Cut the orange in half from top to bottom and slice thinly, saving all the juice and discarding any pips as you go, and place in a small bowl.

Quarter and core the apple and pear, and slice into the bowl. Add the raisins, chopped dates, sliced dried apricots or any other dried or fresh fruit you have at hand and gently stir together.

If not to be eaten immediately, this should be kept covered tightly in the fridge.

Mixed winter juices

Squeeze citrus fruits and mix together – perhaps try a combination of pink grapefruit, orange, blood orange and clementine. Keep refrigerated until ready to serve, then give it a good stir, as the juices will separate soon after squeezing.

Bircher muesli with nuts & apple

SERVES 2
50g rolled oats
100ml whole milk
100g plain yogurt
25g hazelnuts, almonds or walnuts, or a mixture
1 crisp apple
25g sultanas or raisins
Runny honey or maple syrup (optional)

TO SERVE
A selection of fruits, for example:
Spring: banana, pineapple, segments of orange or poached rhubarb
Summer: berries, apricots or peaches (poached, baked or raw)
Autumn and Winter: poached or raw plums, blackberries, poached or
  raw pears, or pieces of poached quince

Mix the rolled oats, milk and plain yogurt together in a bowl and allow
to soak or at least 20–30 minutes. This may be done the night before and
then left in the fridge.

Just before serving, chop the nuts and add to the bowl. Grate the apple,
including the skin, into the mixture as well, adding the sultanas or raisins
at the end. Mix gently to combine, then spoon into 2 bowls and serve
topped with fruits of your choice. Drizzle with honey or maple syrup, if
you like.

Warm porridge with brown sugar

SERVES 1
40g rolled oats
Pinch salt
Approximately 25ml milk

TO SERVE
Brown sugar, maple syrup, honey or cream

Although some prefer to soak the oats in the water overnight, I find that it is just as easy (if a little longer) to make it all on the day.

First, put the rolled oats in a small pan with the pinch of salt and barely cover with 250ml water. Place on a very low heat.

After 5–10 minutes, and occasional stirring, the porridge should have come to a gentle simmer and thickened. Give it a final stir and remove from the heat.

Add a little milk until the consistency is to your liking. Pour into a bowl, sprinkle with brown sugar or drizzle with maple syrup or honey, add cream if you want and eat while warm.

Hot mocha drink with whipped cream

SERVES 1
Coffee – made from freshly ground beans is ideal
200ml whole milk
25g good-quality dark chocolate, chopped or grated
1tbsp double cream, lightly whipped (optional)

Make a very strong coffee in the normal way, using half the normal amount of water, and heat the milk in a small pan.

Place the dark chocolate in a large mug or cup and pour the coffee over, to half fill the cup. Add the hot milk and stir. Top with a spoonful of whipped double cream, if using, and 'eat' with a spoon immediately.

Breakfast... full

Sadly full breakfasts and I hardly ever coincide,
unless I am on holiday. Being in the mountains comes to mind:
glorious cheeses, cream, cured meats, flaky croissants,
seeded rye breads and all that fresh air.
Perhaps there is no better way to start the day,
assuming that you are fortunate enough
to have the time.

Spring and Summer

Kedgeree
Warm ricotta pancakes with maple syrup
Avocado on toasted sour dough with egg and smoked paprika
Open omelette with fresh goat's cheese and herbs

Autumn and Winter

Potato pancake with smoked salmon and soured cream
Sausages, bacon, mushrooms and eggs
Baked eggs, mushrooms and spinach

Kedgeree

This is the most perfect dish for making good use of leftover rice, fish (smoked or fresh), chicken or vegetables. All you need is an onion, a few spices and a little bit of time. However, as with most of the dishes listed here, if cooked from scratch, using freshly prepared ingredients, it can be a revelation. If made fresh, it may be cooled down and left in the fridge for reheating the next day, however, if using ingredients left from previous meals, you need to be careful about reheating leftovers (see pages 28–29).

Although kedgeree is best eaten hot, straight from the pan, it is also delicious served cold in the summer, as a quick midday snack. Simply pack it up in a box with a few salad leaves and a dollop of sour cream or yogurt as dressing, and you will have a meal fit for a king.

SERVES 4–6

3 large free-range or organic eggs
200g basmati or long-grain rice
450g smoked haddock
350ml milk
3 bay leaves
3tbsp vegetable oil
1 large onion, peeled and
  finely diced

1tsp turmeric
3tbsp chopped parsley,
1tbsp chopped coriander, plus a
  few sprigs for garnish
100g sultanas
½ lemon, juice
4 lemon wedges, to serve
Plain yogurt, to serve

Place the eggs in a small pan of boiling water, using a spoon to carefully lower them in. Simmer for 8 minutes, drain and cool under a cold running tap. Peel and cut into quarters.

Cook the rice in a large pan of salted boiling water until tender. This will take approximately 8–10 minutes but it is important to take 1 or »

Spring and Summer

2 grains out of the pan throughout the cooking time to check the doneness. Drain the rice through a sieve, cover and set aside.

Meanwhile, place the smoked haddock in a shallow frying pan and cover with the milk and 350ml water, then add the bay leaves and some freshly ground pepper. Bring to the boil, then immediately turn down to a simmer, cover with a lid or a piece of aluminium foil and continue to poach until the fish flakes easily with a fork and the skin pulls away. This may take up to 15 minutes, depending on the thickness of the fillet, but it is important the fish becomes beautifully tender, not dry, so keep checking the doneness.

Drain the milk away into a small bowl. Using a fork and spoon, first remove and discard the skin, then flake the fish into bite-sized pieces, checking that any remaining bones are removed also.

Heat a large heavy-based pan with the vegetable oil and onion and stir until it starts to sizzle. Turn down the heat and cover with a lid. Cook for 5–10 minutes or until the onion has softened but not browned. Add the spices and a little salt and stir well, continuing to cook for 1–2 minutes until the aromas of the spices are fragrant and fill the kitchen.

Little by little, add the rice to the onion mix, breaking it up gently as it may have started to stick together. Reheat the rice over a medium heat, turning it over together so that the rice is evenly coated in the spicy onion mix. Gently fold the fish into the rice over a gentle heat, tasting as you go and adding a little of the milk if it looks dry. Note that this is not a creamy, liquid risotto-type dish, more a dry, mildly spicy rice dish, which is moistened by the egg yolks and the fish cooking juices. Finally, add the chopped herbs, sultanas and a squeeze of lemon.

Spoon the kedgeree into a warm serving dish and garnish with the egg quarters, sprigs of coriander and lemon wedges. If a little extra juiciness is preferred, a scoop of plain yogurt is a lovely addition.

If using leftovers for this dish, cook the onion and spices as above, and over a medium heat, add the cooked rice, flaked or chopped cooked fish, shredded chicken or chopped cooked vegetables. Stir gently together over the heat until thoroughly reheated, adding a little chicken, fish or vegetable stock if required. Garnish as above and serve immediately. Do not reheat.

Warm ricotta pancakes with maple syrup

These are American or Australian in style rather than British – light and fluffy and perfect for stacking on top of one another and drizzling with maple syrup.

SERVES 4–6–8 DEPENDING ON APPETITES
3 free-range or organic eggs,
  separated
225g ricotta, or plain yogurt
150ml milk
185g plain flour
½tsp bicarbonate of soda
1tbsp sugar
Pinch salt
A little butter, for frying

TO SERVE
Maple syrup or runny honey
Any of the following: chopped
  pecans, sliced banana, berries,
  poached fruit, crème fraîche or
  whipped double cream

Make a batter for the pancakes by whisking the egg yolks together with the ricotta (or yogurt) and milk until smooth. Sift the flour with the other dry ingredients and a pinch of salt into a medium bowl and make a well in the centre. Pour the liquid into the well and very gently start to stir it with a whisk, incorporating a small amount of the flour from the sides, little by little. After a few minutes, the flour will have been amalgamated. Give the batter a brisk whisk to remove any lumps and set aside to rest. (You will need one too, probably.) This could be made the night before if you have time – just leave it covered in the fridge.

Just before cooking, whisk the egg whites in a clean bowl using an electric whisk or mixer, until stiff peaks have formed. Alternatively, this may be done by hand with a large bowl and clean whisk, but this will take a little more time and effort. »

Fold the egg whites into the batter carefully, using a large metal spoon ideally, as you do not want to be too heavy-handed with this. Think light, careful stirs, as you lift the heavy batter up and over the egg whites and carefully blend them together.

Leave on one side in a cool place while you heat the oven to 160°C/ fan oven 140°C/mark 3.

Heat a little butter in a non-stick frying pan until sizzling. Using a small ladle or kitchen spoon, pour a small amount of the batter into the hot pan, making 3 to 4 pancakes at a time. They will cook quite quickly over a medium heat, turning a deep golden colour on the underside as the top starts to set with the heat. Using a palette knife, flip each pancake over carefully, and cook on the other side as before. Once they are nicely brown on both sides, remove to a plate in the warm oven and continue cooking the remaining pancakes as before, adding a little extra butter if the pan looks dry. If the butter burns, remove the pan from the heat and wipe out with kitchen paper or a dishcloth, and start again as before.

If the cooking of individual pancakes is beyond your capabilities (and it can be a bit fiddly at first) make 3 or 4 large pancakes instead as follows:

Heat a small amount of butter in a non-stick frying pan over a medium to high heat, as above, then pour quarter of the batter into the pan all at once, allowing it to spread all over the surface of the pan. Cook the pancake until dark golden underneath and then, once the surface has slightly set, using a fish slice or palette knife, turn it over carefully.

Cook the other side for another 1–2 minutes until golden and then slide the pancake onto a parchment paper-lined baking sheet and cook through for 2–3 minutes in the oven. Continue with the remaining batter as before. Remove the cooked pancakes to a chopping board and slice them into wedges like a cake.

To serve, overlap the pancakes (or wedges) on a warm serving dish, then drizzle with maple syrup or runny honey and, if you wish, finally scatter the pancakes with a selection of nuts or fruit. A dollop of crème fraîche or whipped double cream may also be served on the side.

Avocado on toasted sour dough with egg & smoked paprika

SERVES 2

3 large free-range or organic eggs, room temperature

2 ripe avocados

½ lime, juice

2 large slices sour dough bread

½ bunch watercress, stalks removed, washed and spun dry

Smoked paprika or freshly ground pepper

Gently lower the eggs into a pan of boiling water and cook for 6 minutes. Remove from the pan and run under cold water while peeling carefully.

Place the peeled eggs on one side while the remaining ingredients are prepared.

Cut the avocados in half, remove the stone and scoop out the flesh into a bowl. Season with sea salt and lime juice and mash gently (though not too smooth).

Toast or grill the sour dough slices on both sides, and spread generously with the avocado. Cut each slice into 3 and arrange on a serving plate. Scatter each with watercress leaves, then carefully cut the eggs into quarters and tuck them on top. Sprinkle with a little sea salt and smoked paprika or pepper and serve immediately.

Open omelette with fresh goat's cheese & herbs

Perhaps one of the most classic omelettes in the French repertoire is the omelette aux fines herbes, often given to young recruits in professional kitchens to test their technique and skill. No pressure here though, as the following method leaves the 2-portion omelette open, without the egg being folded into a soft pillowy mound, which many find tricky!

SERVES 2
80g fresh goat's cheese
4 large free-range or organic eggs
75ml milk

1tbsp finely chopped chives
40g butter
Soft herbs, such as parsley, chervil
    and dill, roughly chopped

Turn on the grill/salamander to the highest setting while preparing the ingredients.

Slice the goat's cheese finely or, if it's easier, crumble into small lumps.

Whisk the eggs together until very frothy, with milk, sea salt, freshly ground pepper and finely chopped chives.

Using a small non stick frying pan, heat the butter until sizzling.

Pour the eggs into the hot butter and stir gently while the edges start to become set (approximately 30–60 seconds). Scatter with the goat's cheese, then immediately place the pan under the hot grill. The omelette will puff up around the edges and within a minute or 2, it will be set. Slide the omelette gently onto a warm serving plate and sprinkle with the roughly chopped herbs. Serve with toasts or soft bread and butter.

Potato pancake with smoked salmon & sour cream

Perhaps a rather posh version of 'hash browns' but these deliciously light pancakes are perfect for a weekend breakfast or brunch.

SERVES 6

600g Desiree potatoes, washed, skin on

1 onion, peeled

3 free-range or organic egg whites

2tbsp cornflour

80g butter

80ml vegetable oil

6 large slices smoked salmon

100ml sour cream or crème fraîche

Small bunch chives, finely chopped

Using the wide side of a cheese grater, grate the potatoes into a bowl, then the onion in the same way, and mix together. Scatter these over a clean tea towel, then roll up tightly, squeezing out the excess moisture gently but firmly.

Tip the potato mix into a dry bowl and add the egg whites and cornflour, mixing thoroughly with a little salt and freshly ground pepper.

Heat the oven to 180°C/fan oven 160°C/mark 4.

In a wide heavy-based frying pan, heat half the butter and half the oil over a medium to high heat until sizzling. Spoon the mix into the pan using a dessert spoon, flattening the tops a little. Fry until golden brown underneath (approximately 2–3 minutes), then carefully flip them over to cook on the other side. Once they are crisp on both sides and cooked through, remove them to an ovenproof plate, lined with kitchen paper. Keep them in the warm oven while the remaining pancakes are being fried.

Serve the pancakes as soon as possible, topped with the smoked salmon and a scoop of sour cream, sprinkled generously with chives.

Autumn and WINTER

Sausages, bacon, mushrooms & eggs

SERVES 4
2 tbsp vegetable oil
8 sausages
8 rashers bacon (optional)
4 large free-range or organic eggs

3 large field mushrooms, peeled
and sliced thickly across
8 slices bread of your choice
Mustard and tomato ketchup,
to serve

Heat the oven to 165°C/fan oven 145°C/mark 3. Place a large, flat pan over a medium heat with a little vegetable oil, and cook the sausages until a deep golden brown on all sides. Remove to a dish in the warm oven.

Add the bacon, if using, to the hot pan and fry until crisp on both sides. Remove with tongs and place in the oven with the sausages.

Next place the thick slices of mushroom, cut side down, into the pan and fry until starting to turn golden brown. Flip over with tongs and cook until the other sides are golden brown.

Turn off the oven and place the serving plates inside to warm gently. Arrange the warm sausages (and bacon) in the mushroom pan in such a way as to be easily portioned – so that they are all evenly distributed with the mushroom slices.

Carefully crack the eggs one by one into the pan, in among the other ingredients, so that they too are evenly spaced. Cook over a medium heat so that the egg whites do not cook too quickly. Meanwhile, toast the slices of bread and place in the oven with the plates to keep warm.

Serve as soon as the eggs are set to your liking, and they have 'joined up' the sausages, bacon and mushrooms. Put the pan in the middle of the table, on a heatproof mat, and serve by carving up the sections of sausages, bacon and eggs evenly.

Serve with the toast, mustard and ketchup.

Baked eggs, mushrooms & spinach

SERVES 4
150g young spinach leaves
200g mushrooms
3tbsp olive oil

4 large organic or free-range eggs
1tbsp chopped chives
50g butter
50g soft goat's cheese (optional)

Heat the oven to 170°C/fan oven 150°C/mark 3 and boil the kettle.

Wash the spinach well in lots of cold water, and remove the stalks. When asked how many times the water should be changed while washing spinach, I always answer 'until it is clean!' Spinach is notoriously difficult to clean properly, as it is usually grown in very fine soil, which can cling to the folds in the leaves. However, as the leaves are relatively delicate, you need to wash them with care and a light touch.

Slice the mushrooms finely and cook in a frying pan over a high heat with 2tbsp of the olive oil, sea salt and freshly ground pepper. Once they have softened in the heat and started to release their juices, remove the mushrooms with a slotted spoon to a small bowl and leave on one side.

In the same pan, add the remaining 1tbsp olive oil to the juices, then the spinach, a little salt and pepper, then cover with a lid. Wilt the leaves over a medium heat, stirring occasionally for 2–3 minutes. Remove with a slotted spoon, to a small bowl, leaving the juices behind.

Choose 4 ramekins (or 1 medium-sized shallow dish) and place the drained spinach in the bases, divided evenly. Next place the mushrooms on top, again divided evenly, then crack an egg into each. (If using 1 dish for 4 people, make small indentations in the mushroom/spinach mix so that the eggs sit comfortably, but separately within.) Sprinkle with salt and pepper, chives and a sliver of butter. Place the ramekins in a small roasting tin and carefully pour the boiling water into the tin, around them, to approximately 1cm deep. Carefully slide the tray into the oven and bake for 10–12 minutes or until the eggs have cooked to your liking. For a slightly more robust meal, add a slice or two of soft goat's cheese to the topping halfway through the cooking time.

Serve with buttered toasts or freshly baked soda bread (see page 77).

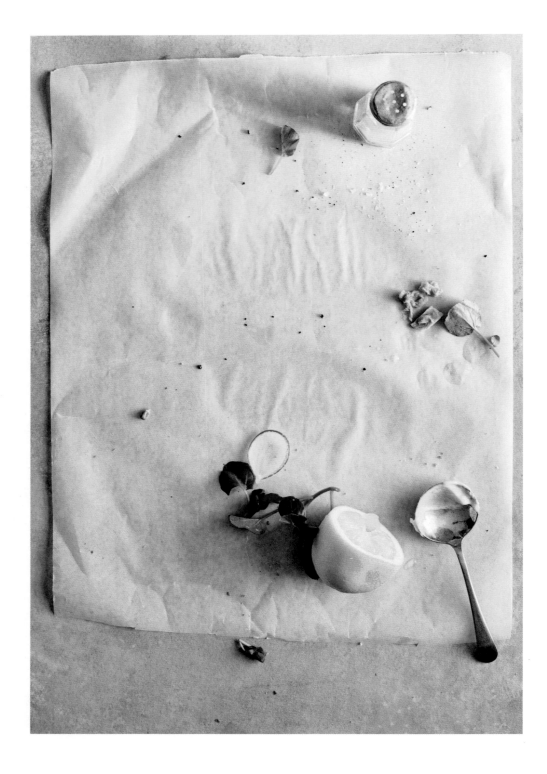

Lunch... on the run

Here are a selection of sandwiches – perfect for a student at a desk,
with a looming deadline perhaps. Simple and relatively quick
to assemble and wrap, then tasty and nourishing to eat a little later.
Or, if time allows and you are working from home, rustle up the divinely
soft eggs with asparagus. In the cooler months, leftovers of the galette or
pissaladière make the perfect transportable picnic or midday snack.

Spring and Summer

Roasted chicken and mozzarella open sandwiches with basil
Soda bread with cheese, pickles and celery
Tuna sandwich with radish and cucumber
Scrambled eggs with spring onion and asparagus

Autumn and Winter

Pumpkin, blue cheese and walnut galette
Vine tomato, parsley and cracked wheat salad
Pissaladière

Roasted chicken & mozzarella open sandwiches with basil

Although this would make a lovely picnic item, it is best to eat at home with a plate and a napkin, as the toppings are likely to go everywhere, unless you are very careful!

MAKES 4

4 slices good bread, sour dough perhaps
2 heaped tbsp mayonnaise (see page 79)
A few small salad leaves of your choice
300g roasted chicken, shredded (see page 172)
2 balls buffalo mozzarella, drained
A few vine tomatoes, halved
A few basil leaves
Olive oil
½ lemon or lime, cut into wedges

Toast the bread on both sides, if you like. Lay the slices next to each other on a clean tabletop or chopping board, and spread generously with mayonnaise. Scatter the salad leaves on top, then the shredded chicken.

Cut the mozzarella into cubes or wedges, then pile these on top with the tomatoes and basil leaves. Season with sea salt, freshly ground pepper, a drizzle of olive oil and a squeeze of lemon or lime. Serve immediately.

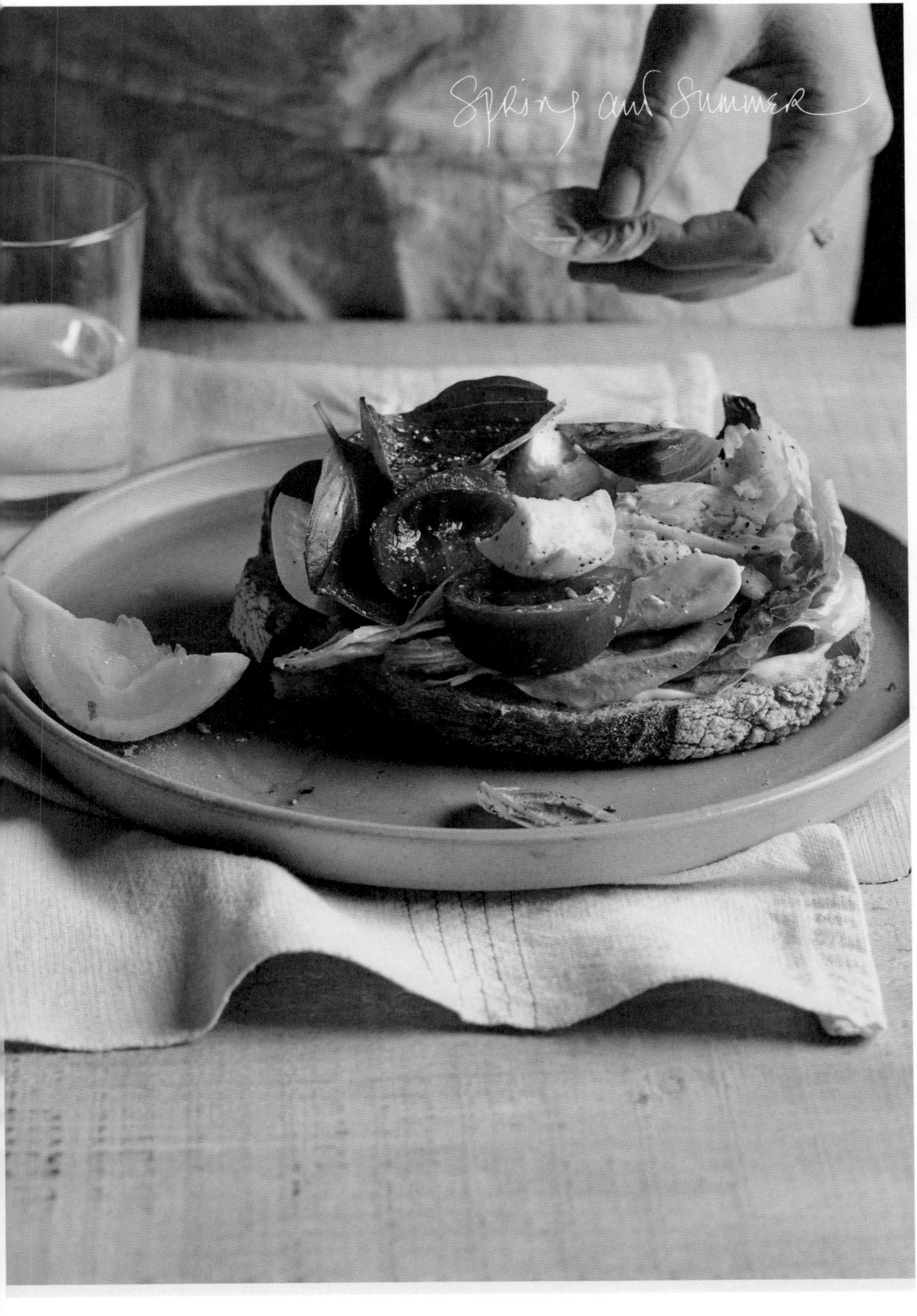
Spring and Summer

Soda bread with cheese, pickles & celery

Soda bread is probably one of the simplest and quickest breads in the world to make, as it does not require any kneading or proofing at all. However, it should ideally be made with good-quality flour, perhaps one from a local miller, or a wholegrain variety, to make it special. Although best eaten straight from the oven, you can also make this the day before, or in the morning, and then serve it when you get in for lunch. Or if it is a beautiful day, take this into the open air, as a picnic with some fruit for dessert.

MAKES 1 LOAF
300g plain white flour
100g wholemeal flour, plus a little extra for dusting
50g rolled oats
1 level tsp bicarbonate of soda
1 level tsp brown sugar
1 level tsp seas salt
1 large tbsp plain yogurt
350ml buttermilk or whole milk
A little vegetable oil
A selection of cheeses, pickles, chutneys, celery heart and radishes,
  to serve

Heat the oven to 230°C/fan oven 210°C/mark 8.

Place the flours, rolled oats, bicarbonate of soda, sugar and salt in a large bowl. In a separate bowl, whisk the yogurt with the buttermilk or milk. Pour the liquid into the large bowl and mix together with a fork until it is all well amalgamated.

Remove the dough from the bowl and mix together by hand on a clean tabletop until it has formed a smoothish ball. »

Smear a little oil on a baking sheet and place the dough in the middle.

Sprinkle the top with a little extra wholemeal flour then, using the handle of a wooden spoon, make a 'cross' indentation on the top of the loaf, pushing the spoon handle down approximately halfway through the dough. As my friend Darina Allen of Ballymaloe Cookery School in County Cork, Ireland, says with authority, this action 'lets the fairies out'.

Bake for 15 minutes, then turn the heat down to 200°C/fan oven 180°C/ mark 6 and bake for 30 more minutes or until the loaf has risen a little and turned golden at the edges. When cooked, it should sound hollow when tapped underneath.

While traditional breads are better not eaten straight from the oven, this one certainly is. There is nothing much better than eating a chunk of warm soda bread (broken along its indentations) with salted butter and a chunk of salty cheese, such as Cheddar, Lancashire, Cheshire, Coolea or Isle of Mull Cheddar with the heart of celery (leaves attached), a few radishes, a scoop of sweet-sour chutney or pickled gherkins or onions.

Tuna sandwich with radish & cucumber

This sandwich can be made in the normal way or 'open', as in the delicious Danish tradition, and you can either use toasted bread or fresh slices. The mayonnaise binds the ingredients together and holds the ingredients in place.

Hellman's makes a great product, and some professional cooks use it instead of going to the trouble of making their own mayonnaise – as do many home cooks. However, if you are of a mind to go the extra mile, both in flavour and self worth, try making your own. Once the knack is found, the scary element will be a thing of the past. As with many tasks in the kitchen, making mayonnaise is easier if you ask a friend to help, as it is important to be pouring slowly and beating fast at the same time.

One point to remember is that the by-product of making your own mayonnaise is of course egg whites – and for this reason I suggest making meringues as a dessert (see page 131). These do not have to be made on the same day as the mayonnaise, as the whites can safely stay in the fridge, covered, for up to 3 days. Once baked, the meringues will last up to 2–3 weeks stored in an airtight container.

SERVES 4

FOR THE MAYONNAISE
2 free-range or organic
  eggs
1tsp Dijon mustard
100ml olive oil
150ml vegetable oil
½ lemon, juice

FOR THE SANDWICHES
1 can good-quality tuna, in brine or oil
¼ small cucumber (approximately 5cm long)
A few salad leaves or ½ bunch watercress,
  stalks removed, washed and spun dry
A few radishes, washed, leaves removed
8 slices granary bread (see page 39) or
  wholemeal or sourdough
½ lemon, juice

For the mayonnaise

Break the eggs carefully and separate the yolks from the whites into 2 containers. If a yolk breaks, use a piece of shell to scoop out the yolk from the white. Remember – a bit of white in the yolk is fine, but not the other way round.

Place the yolks in a medium-sized bowl and mix in the mustard using a wooden spoon or a whisk. Holding the bowl firmly with one hand, beat the oils in literally drop by drop. It will mean stopping and starting a lot while the drops are added between each addition, but the emulsion must be smooth and thick each time before the next addition of oil.

Once half the oil has been added, and providing you are feeling confident, the remaining oil may be added in slightly larger quantities, but the aim of this exercise is to allow the oil to be continually emulsified by the egg yolks throughout. If the mixture 'splits' or curdles, do not worry. Simply restart the process with a clean bowl and a fresh egg yolk. Very carefully drip the curdled liquid into the yolk, drop by drop as before, whisking continuously until it becomes thick and glossy.

Finally, add some salt, freshly ground pepper and the lemon juice, taste and leave on one side. The mayonnaise will stay fresh for up to 5 days if covered and stored in the fridge.

You may use the following additions to adapt the flavours for other dishes:

For a strong mustard mayonnaise, add 1 heaped tsp Dijon or wholegrain mustard.

For tarragon or basil mayonnaise, add 1tbsp chopped tarragon or basil leaves.

For anchovy mayonnaise, add 5–6 finely chopped anchovy fillets.

For green mayonnaise, add 2tbsp very finely chopped soft herbs, such as parsley, chives, chervil or tarragon. (Purists push the finished mayonnaise through a sieve before serving, so that only the green juices remain.)

For garlic mayonnaise, add 1 clove garlic crushed to a cream and a squeeze of lemon.

For tartare sauce, add 1tbsp chopped gherkins, ½tbsp each of capers, parsley and chives and a squeeze of lemon.

For the sandwiches

Drain the tuna and roughly break up the pieces. Slice the cucumber thinly and shred the lettuce leaves or pick the thick stalks away from the watercress. Slice the radishes finely.

Lay the fresh (or freshly toasted) bread slices on a chopping board. Spread thickly with mayonnaise, and scatter half the slices with the salad leaves. Divide the tuna among these and top with the cucumber and radish slices. Season with salt, pepper and a squeeze of lemon. Finally, place the remaining slices on top, mayonnaise-side downwards, and press together gently. With a serrated or sharp knife, cut into halves or quarters and serve.

Alternatively, if you do not want such a filling amount of bread, simply use 4 slices of bread or toast, spread liberally with mayonnaise as before, and pile the ingredients on top attractively, finishing with a squeeze of lemon. Serve as an open sandwich.

If this will be a picnic or packed lunch, wrap each sandwich carefully in greaseproof paper or clingfilm. In this way, they will last nicely for a few hours in the fridge or in a cool bag. Remember to take some kitchen roll to use as napkins.

Scrambled eggs with spring onion & asparagus

This makes a perfect breakfast also – served with a pot of coffee or tea and freshly squeezed juice on the side.

SERVES 4

1 bunch green asparagus
  (12–15 spears)
4 thick slices sour dough or
  granary bread (see page 39)

8 free-range or organic eggs
200ml milk
50g butter
½ bunch spring onions, trimmed
  at both ends, finely sliced

Wash, trim away and discard the woody bases of the asparagus and blanch the spears in boiling, salted water for 1–2 minutes, then drain and leave on one side.

Toast the bread on both sides.

Using a fork, whisk the eggs lightly with salt and freshly ground pepper and the milk until lightly foaming. Add the sliced spring onions.

Heat the butter in a non-stick pan until liquid and softly sizzling. Pour in the eggs and stir over a medium heat until cooked to your liking – approximately 2–3 minutes. Do you like them smooth and runny or with large lumps of soft curds within a creamy, eggy sauce? For smooth eggs, keep stirring continuously; for the latter, just occasionally scrape the cooked curds away from the edge of the pan, until the scramble is to your liking.

Place the toasts on warm plates, then pile the asparagus on top, spears pointing in the same direction. Pour the scrambled eggs over the spears, leaving the points exposed, and serve immediately.

Pumpkin, blue cheese & walnut galette

SERVES 4–6

FOR THE PASTRY
200g plain flour, plus extra for dusting
100g butter, cubed
A little chilled water

FOR THE FILLING
2tbsp olive oil
1 onion, peeled and diced
500g pumpkin, peel removed and chopped into hazelnut-sized pieces
1tsp finely chopped thyme or rosemary
150g blue cheese, such as Stilton, Beenleigh Blue, Roquefort or similar,
  cut into small dice or gently crumbled. If a less strong cheese is
  preferred, choose Cheddar, Lancashire or Cheshire
1tbsp chopped walnuts

First, make the pastry. Place the flour and butter in a bowl with a pinch each of sea salt and freshly ground pepper. Using just the fingertips, rub the butter into the flour, lifting it up as you do so. Keep working the mixture until the butter has been amalgamated into the flour and the mass looks like soft white breadcrumbs.

Next, add the chilled water and use a fork to bring the pastry together. Tip the contents of the bowl onto a clean table or board and gently but firmly push it into a ball, trying to handle it as little as possible. If it feels sticky, dust it with a little flour, or if it feels dry and refuses to come together, add a further splash of water and then knead it gently. Wrap the ball of pastry in clingfilm and chill in the fridge for at least 30 minutes.

Meanwhile, prepare the filling. Heat the olive oil over a medium heat in a shallow frying pan, add the onion and fry until it starts to soften (approximately 3–4 minutes). Add the chopped pumpkin and continue to cook, stirring occasionally until it starts to soften at the edges. »

Autumn and Winter

Season with salt and pepper and add the chopped thyme or rosemary. Remove from the heat and tip the contents of the pan onto a large plate. Spread it out as flat as possible to allow it to cool quickly.

Using a rolling pin (or a straight-sided bottle), roll out the pastry with a sprinkling of flour to prevent it from sticking to both the table and the rolling pin. It should be shaped as a disc approximately 30cm across and 2–3mm thick. Do not worry too much about the shape at this stage – it does not have to be a perfect circle.

Using clean fingers or a piece of kitchen paper, smear a baking sheet with a little vegetable oil, then carefully lift the pastry up and lay it in the centre. Heat the oven to 175°C/fan oven 155°C/mark 4.

Once the vegetables have cooled, drain away the juices, if any, then pile them into the centre of the pastry, leaving a rim of at least 2cm around the edge. Flatten the vegetables a little so that they are level. Next, fold the rim of pastry onto itself, a few centimetres at a time, thus 'crimping' and folding the edges as you work your way around the circumference. The vegetables should now be surrounded by a shallow wall of pastry around the edge.

Bake for 20–25 minutes or until the pastry is firm and golden brown in colour. Carefully remove the sheet from the oven and dot the cheese evenly over the top, then scatter with the chopped walnuts. Continue to bake for 5–6 minutes or until the cheese has started to melt and the pastry is firm to the touch.

Remove the galette from the oven and allow to cool for a few minutes before sliding it off the baking sheet and onto a chopping board or serving plate. You may find that a fish slice or palette knife could help to ease the galette off the tray.

Slice and serve warm immediately, or cold the next day with a salad of bitter leaves, or with cold meats if a more robust meal is required.

Vine tomato, parsley & cracked wheat salad

Contrary to many a cracked wheat recipe, I do not believe that cracked wheat needs soaking or cooking before using – far better in my mind, and more flavourful, to soak it in the juices of the dish. Choose the ripest tomatoes you can find – a variety of colours is good, but above all they need to be full of juice and full of flavour.

SERVES 4-6
400g tomatoes, ideally large plum or 'beefsteak' variety
½ cucumber
1 large lemon, juice
170g cracked wheat
1tbsp pine nuts
4tbsp olive oil
2tbsp chopped parsley
1tbsp chopped mint
1tbsp chopped chives or finely sliced spring onion tops
1 small pomegranate (optional)

Although time consuming, I prefer to peel and de-seed the tomatoes first. If this 'perfectionist' approach is favoured, peel the tomatoes as described on page 24. Cut each one into quarters and, while saving all the juices, scoop the seeds away with a small, sharp knife, leaving the 'petals' of the tomato to one side. Cut the petals into small dice, add to a large bowl and strain the seeds and juice over through a small sieve. Discard the peel and seeds. Alternatively, if you prefer, simply cut the whole tomatoes into small dice, saving all the juices as you do so.

Cut the cucumber in half lengthwise, then each half into 4 again lengthwise, and chop across into small bite-size chunks. Place the cucumber in the bowl with the tomatoes and mix with sea salt, freshly ground pepper, lemon juice, a splash of cold water and the cracked » wheat. Toss together, cover and leave for at least 2 hours to marinate, stirring occasionally. The salad may be left in the fridge, covered, for up to 24 hours.

In a small saucepan, heat the pine nuts with the olive oil and stir over a medium heat until golden. Leave on one side to cool completely.

To serve, stir the herbs, pine nuts and olive oil into the cracked wheat, taste for seasoning and pile onto a serving dish.

An addition of pomegranate seeds is lovely sprinkled on the top. Simply cut the pomegranate through the equator then, holding the cut sides down over a bowl, one at a time, knock the skin with a rolling pin or small hammer. The seeds will simply drop out into the bowl – but do make sure that you do not spill one drop of the precious juice. Pick out the white membrane that may still be attached to the seeds. Sprinkle the beautiful seeds over the salad, including the saved juice.

Pissaladière

A 'classically correct' pissaladière should of course include anchovy, but instead I have chosen to use 'fillets' of roasted red peppers to create a vegetarian version of this lovely dish.

At our bakery we make a fabulous all-butter puff pastry, which is used for our now famous sausage rolls year round, and in the summer for our very pretty raspberry and crème Chantilly millefeuilles. However, as this is one of the most difficult pastries in the repertoire to make, I believe that for most of us, buying it in 'ready-made' is nothing to be ashamed of! Most good supermarkets now offer a more than acceptable range of ready-to-roll pastry, and puff pastry is one of the most popular.

SERVES 4–6 DEPENDING ON APPETITES
400g puff pastry
75ml olive oil, plus extra for the peppers
2tsp chopped thyme
2 large onions, peeled and very finely sliced
1 large red pepper
A large handful good-quality black olives, halved and pitted

First, roll the puff pastry to approximately 15cm square, dusting the rolling pin and table with a little flour to prevent sticking. Place on a baking sheet and leave to chill in the fridge while the remaining ingredients are assembled.

Heat the olive oil in a heavy-based pan with the thyme until gently sizzling, then add the onion and cook over a medium to high heat until the slices are golden brown and soft. Season with sea salt and freshly ground pepper, then tip them into a sieve over a bowl to catch the juices, and allow to drain.

Cut the sides away from the red pepper, in 3 or 4 pieces depending on the shape, then cut each piece in half lengthwise. Using the juices from the onion, plus a little extra olive oil, gently cook the peppers in a shallow pan with a lid until soft, but not coloured. Remove from the heat and allow to cool, covered. Once cool enough to handle, carefully pull the skins away and discard along with the juices. Cut the peppers into long thin strips and leave on one side.

Heat the oven to 200°C/fan oven 180°C/mark 6.

Remove the pastry from the fridge and prick all over (not the edges) with a fork, as this will allow the steam to escape during baking. Trim and neaten the edges with a sharp knife.

Spread the cooled, drained onion slices over the pastry, leaving a rim of 1cm around the edges uncovered. Place on the top shelf of the oven and bake for 20–25 minutes or until puffed and golden. Remove from the oven and place the red pepper fillets in a criss-cross pattern over the top, then fill the 'gaps' of the peppers with the pitted olive halves. Turning the tray around (for even baking), continue to cook for a further 5–7 minutes or until the pastry is a deep golden brown.

Remove from the oven and slide on to a cooling rack so that the underneath can be checked. The pastry should be crisp throughout, even in the centre!

Slice and serve immediately (or cold the next day) with a lovely salad of bitter leaves.

Lunch... no time restrictions

Sometimes it just happens – that lovely moment
when everything feels just right. A lunch that starts at no particular
time, then hardly finishes at all. It could possibly even blend
into supper, with friends so relaxed and well fed
that they hardly notice the time!
NB It is very important however that throughout all this,
the cook is looked after, and stays calm and organised
until everyone has gone home!

Spring and Summer

Cold poached ham with raw vegetables and mayonnaise
A lovely ham and vegetable broth
Hamburgers with guacamole, tomato and cucumber salad
Marinated fresh anchovies
Pea and celery risotto with pea leaves

Autumn and Winter

Chicory, grape and Brussels sprout salad with hazelnuts
Braised neck of lamb with spices, orange, rosemary and lentils
Winter slaw with red cabbage, parsnip and pomegranate
Savoury tart filled with leek and field mushrooms

Spring and Summer

Cold poached ham with raw vegetables & mayonnaise

Most butchers will sell cooked ham in one piece or sliced to order in front of you.

Alternatively, you may wish to cook the ham yourself, thus saving money (but not time). If this is the case, ideally you need to start the process 2 days in advance. Choose the vegetables from the market and wash them well. You will just need a small handful of each one.

SERVES 4–6
1 piece salted ham hock or collar, approximately 600g
A few bay leaves
1 onion, peeled and halved, each half pierced with a few cloves
2 sticks celery
2 carrots, peeled
A few peppercorns
A selection of vegetables, such as radishes, carrot, fennel, heart
  of celery or asparagus

TO SERVE
Mustard mayonnaise (see page 79)
Pickled gherkins, onions or chutney

Soak the ham overnight in cold water to release the excess salt. Drain the ham and place it in a large pan, cover well with fresh water and add the bay leaves, pierced onion, celery, carrots and peppercorns.

Bring up to a gentle simmer and cook, covered with a lid, for up to 1½ hours, occasionally skimming the liquid to remove any scum that rises to the surface. If the water level reduces below the top of the ham, simply top up with a little water from time to time during the cooking.

When a small sharp knife or skewer pierces the meat easily, remove the pan from the heat. In a cool part of the kitchen, allow the ham to cool in the liquid for 1–2 hours.

When the ham is cold, remove it to a chopping board, trim away and discard the rind and excess fat. Strain the liquid and keep well covered in the fridge for a later use (such as a soup, risotto, broth or sauce) for up to 3 days. Retain the celery and carrots also, as these would make a lovely addition to a soup (see page 100) or risotto (see page 107).

Next, prepare the vegetables as follows:

Radishes may be left whole, with some of the good leaves attached.

Carrots should be washed and peeled, then cut lengthwise into quarters or sixteenths (depending on the size), including 1cm of green stalk if present.

Fennel should be washed, then cut into quarters and break apart the leaves. Cut into evenly sized pieces.

Celery should be trimmed at the base. Cut the heart into equal width sticks, leaving the leaves attached.

Asparagus should be washed and cut into long slices on the angle if small, or in half lengthwise if thicker.

To serve, slice the ham as thinly as possible, across (not along) the grain of the meat, and place on one side of a platter. Arrange the raw vegetables around decoratively, keeping colours and shapes in mind as you do so. Place a large pot of mustard mayonnaise on one side. Serve with pickled gherkins, onions or chutney. A glass of cider works particularly well as an accompaniment.

A lovely ham & vegetable broth –
for using up the trimmings
of the ham

SERVES 2–3
750ml ham broth
The cooked vegetables, approximately 4–5tbsp
The ham trimmings, approximately 2–3tbsp
Celery, parsley or spinach leaves, or a mixture of all, washed and torn
  into small pieces.

Bring the broth up to the boil and skim away any impurities that float to
the top, then turn the heat down to a gentle simmer.

Meanwhile, cut the cooked vegetables into small dice and add to the pot.

Next, trim away any excess fat from the ham, then slice or dice the ham
trimmings and add to the pot.

Finally, stir in the chopped celery, parsley or spinach leaves, taste and
then ladle into warm soup bowls.

Serve with bread or a baked potato and a salad. For a more robust soup,
add cooked pasta, pulses or rice of your choice or cooked grains such as
spelt, barley or freekeh.

Hamburgers with guacamole, tomato & cucumber salad

To make the ideal hamburgers, you need to first find someone who has a charcoal grill or barbecue – even a little Japanese hibachi grill sitting on a back doorstep. You will achieve the best flavour by singeing the edges of the meat over the hot embers. The second best method is to place the burgers under the grill on full heat in an oven, but this can seriously ruin a perfectly clean oven in a few minutes. Lastly, the burgers could be cooked to an acceptable crustiness simply in a hot heavy-based griddle or frying pan.

SERVES 4

FOR THE HAMBURGERS
750g lean beef or lamb mince
A little finely chopped green or red chilli (or use pepper)
1tbsp chopped parsley or celery leaves
1tbsp finely chopped onion or spring onion (the white part)
½tsp finely chopped marjoram or thyme leaves
Pinch sea salt

FOR THE GUACAMOLE
2 small avocados, ripe but not discoloured
1 large lime, juice
Finely chopped chilli, to taste
1tsp finely chopped coriander leaves
1tbsp finely chopped spring onion (the green part)

FOR THE TOMATO AND CUCUMBER SALAD
3 ripe tomatoes (approximately 400g)
½ small cucumber
Finely chopped chilli, to taste (or use freshly ground pepper)
Splash olive oil
Splash lemon or lime juice
1tbsp finely chopped spring onion (the green part)

TO SERVE
Lettuce leaves
Warm burger buns, baps or toasts
Mayonnaise, mustard or tomato ketchup

First, make and shape the hamburgers. Place the beef or lamb in a bowl with the remaining ingredients. Mix thoroughly, either with a wooden spoon or by hand. Divide the mixture evenly into 4 and shape into patties by cupping the mixture in between your hands. Make sure they are smooth all over, as cracks in the mixture are liable to break open when cooking. Leave, covered, on a plate in the fridge.

Meanwhile, make the guacamole. Cut the avocados in half and use a spoon to scoop out the flesh from the skin into a bowl. Using a fork, mash until almost smooth, then add the lime juice, a little sea salt, the chilli, coriander and spring onion and mix together well. Taste – it should be spicy and citrusy. Leave, covered, in the fridge until ready to serve.

Finally, make the salad. Cut the tomatoes into cubes, then cut the cucumber into the same size. Season with salt, chilli or pepper and a splash of olive oil and lemon or lime juice. Mix together well so that all is coated in the dressing, taste and pile into a small serving bowl.

Heat your grill, barbecue or pan to cook the hamburgers to your required doneness. Most people are happy with a medium-rare finish and this is best achieved by searing both sides of the burgers over (or under) the highest heat you can create. Once the outside is charred to your liking, move the burgers to a slightly cooler part of the grill to allow the meat to cook through. After 2–3 minutes on each side, the burgers should have reached the correct temperature inside, but all grills are different, and the thickness of the patties will also differ.

To test the doneness, remove a burger from the heat and very gently break a small section of the meat away, so that the inside is partially exposed. If it seems too raw, place back on or under the heat for a minute or 2 longer. Alternatively, press lightly on the top of a hamburger with a spoon or a fork. If the juices run pink, they will be ready. Allow to rest for a minute in a warm place while you place the bowls of guacamole and tomato salad on the table with a selection of lettuce leaves next to them. Serve with the buns, mayonnaise, mustard or ketchup.

Marinated fresh anchovies

As it was for Samuel, my love of food and farmers' markets was triggered during family holidays in France from the 1960s with my parents and 2 brothers. The older we became, the further south we would travel each summer, and en route, we would choose our picnic lunches from the village *traiteurs*, *boulangeries* and street markets. Once we had reached our destination, usually a modest family-run restaurant with rooms, close to the sea, we would start exploring. Not only the rock pools and the ice cream shops but also the menus. There we always found something different to taste – artichokes, courgettes and weirdly shaped tomatoes, huge bowls of mussels, calf's brain...

I am not sure when or where I ate my first raw anchovy – could it have been then, in Brittany, sitting by a fishing port in the sunshine? Or could it have been much later, in California, at the wonderful Zuni restaurant in San Francisco? Here, anchovy fillets are often served as a pre-starter, drizzled with olive oil and a scattering of finely sliced celery.

Wherever it was, I still love them – and whilst to the uninitiated, the thought of an anchovy, let alone a raw one, is something to be scared of, I am a keen persuader, and would love to think that this simple method of preparation could help convert a few antis...

Use this recipe only when the freshest of anchovies are available to you. They should be firm to the touch, with glistening eyes and scales, and should have a fresh, appealing smell of the sea.

FOR 4 AS A STARTER

12 fresh anchovies
2 small lemons
Small celery sticks from the heart, including the leaves
Olive oil

TO SERVE
Bread or sour dough toasts and butter
Radishes
Olives

Rinse the anchovies under a cold running tap, gently rubbing away the scales. Make a small incision in the belly and remove the innards. Rinse again under cold running water. Dry the fish with kitchen paper and lay them on a chopping board. With a small knife, slide the blade over the backbone, from the head to the tail, removing the fillet from the bone with one easy stroke. Turn the fish over and repeat on the other side. Once they are all filleted, wipe them gently with kitchen paper and check that there are no bones.

Lay the fillets like soldiers on a flat serving dish, silver skin side up, and sprinkle with the juice of 1 lemon. Cover and chill in the fridge for at least 20 minutes.

Slice the celery finely on the angle, including the leaves.

Remove the dish from the fridge, drizzle the fillets with a little olive oil, some freshly ground pepper and scatter with the sliced celery. Cut the remaining lemon into 8 wedges and place around the dish.

Serve chilled, with bread and butter or sour dough toasts, radishes, olives and a lovely glass of rosé.

Pea & celery risotto with pea leaves

This recipe works very well using fish stock, but I prefer not to use cheese with fish – this is a personal preference, so see what works best for you and decide for yourself.

SERVES 4-6

600ml vegetable, fish, chicken or
  ham stock
4tbsp olive oil
80g butter
1tsp finely chopped thyme
1 onion, peeled and finely diced
1 stick celery, finely diced
½ bulb fennel, finely diced

250g arborio or carnaroli rice
1 glass dry white wine
250g fresh or frozen peas
  (defrosted)
A handful pea leaves, rocket
  or parsley
75g grated Parmesan or fresh goat's
  cheese (or a mixture of both),
  plus 20g extra Parmesan, to serve

Gently bring the stock to a simmer in a small pan.

Meanwhile, place the olive oil, butter and thyme in a medium-sized, heavy-based pan and heat until starting to sizzle. Add the onion, celery and fennel and cook until they start to soften but not colour. Add the rice, season with sea salt and freshly ground pepper and cook over a medium heat until the oils have been absorbed, but do not allow the rice to colour. Add the wine and stir well for 1–2 minutes while it is absorbed by the rice.

Little by little, add the warm stock over a low heat, stirring from time to time to prevent it from sticking to the base of the pan. This will take up to 15 minutes. If using fresh peas, add them halfway through the cooking time. Once the rice is cooked to your liking, add the pea leaves and the frozen peas (if using), then check the consistency. It should be soupy but not too liquid, and the grains of rice should be part of the liquid, not separated from it.

Remove the pan from the heat, stir in the cheese(s) and taste for seasoning. Allow the risotto to settle for 30–60 seconds before pouring into a warm dish and serving with a little extra grated Parmesan on the side.

Chicory, grape & Brussels sprout salad with hazelnuts

A lovely alternative to the sprout is sprouting purple curly kale, sometimes called kale sprouts. Look out for them in the farmers' markets – and some supermarkets now carry them too.

SERVES 4

FOR THE SALAD
2 heads Belgian endive (chicory)
10–12 Brussels sprouts or a large
  handful kale sprouts
1 bunch watercress, land cress or
  young spinach
Small bunch green or black grapes,
  halved, pips removed

FOR THE DRESSING
1tsp Dijon mustard
1tsp wholegrain mustard
½ lemon, juice
4tsp good olive oil
A few sultanas
A few sliced or chopped hazelnuts
  (or walnuts if unavailable)

Slice across the endive slightly on the angle into thin strips, and place in a large bowl. With a sharp knife, slice the Brussels sprouts or kale sprouts as finely as possible (they are to be eaten raw, so the finer the better) and add to the endive.

Pick, wash and spin dry the watercress, land cress or spinach, discarding the thick stalks. To store in the fridge, the leaves could be simply covered in a bowl with damp kitchen paper.

Make the dressing in a bowl by whisking the mustards, lemon juice and olive oil with sea salt and freshly ground pepper until smooth, then add the sultanas and nuts. Tip in the sprouts and endive and gently mix, along with the grapes.

Finally, fold the watercress or spinach into the bowl, so that the dressing lightly coats all the ingredients. Tip gently into the serving bowl or dish and serve immediately.

Autumn and Winter

Braised neck of lamb with spices, orange, rosemary & lentils

SERVES 4–6
700g lamb neck fillets – ask the butcher to trim most of the fat
1tbsp plain flour
½tsp ground cumin
½tsp ground coriander seeds
1tsp finely chopped rosemary
1 large onion, peeled
1 stick celery
½ bulb fennel
1 large carrot, peeled
1 orange, peel and juice
500ml chicken, lamb, beef or vegetable stock
1 glass wine, any colour
100g brown lentils, Puy or Castelluccio are ideal

TO SERVE
1tbsp roughly chopped celery leaves
1tbsp roughly chopped parsley
Plain yogurt or sour cream and/or bread of your choice

Heat the oven to 170°C/fan oven 150°C/mark 3. Cut the neck fillets into equal-sized pieces approximately the size of walnuts. Place these in a bowl, sprinkle with the flour, spices and chopped rosemary and season with sea salt and freshly ground pepper, then jumble together.

Cut the vegetables into evenly sized pieces, sliced or cubed as you wish. (See pages 22–23 for instructions.)

Place the orange peel and juice in a small saucepan with the stock and wine. Bring to a rolling boil, then turn off the heat and leave on one side.

Place the meat in an ovenproof dish, scatter over the lentils and cover with the vegetables. Pour the hot liquid over, then cover with a tight-fitting lid or piece of aluminium foil. »

Cook in the oven for 80–90 minutes or until the meat and lentils are tender and the juices flavourful. The easiest way to check is to carefully dig into the bottom of the dish and pull out a piece of meat. Try to pull it apart with a fork – if it is resistant, return to the oven and continue to cook for a few more minutes. If the level of juice has reduced below the level of the meat, top up with a little more warm stock or water from a kettle.

When the meat is cooked to your liking, turn off the oven and warm the plates or bowls inside.

Allow the braise to sit for 10–20 minutes in the cooling oven before skimming away any fat that may have risen to the surface.

Stir the celery or parsley leaves into the dish, gently mixing the lentils and vegetables with the meat. Serve with a dollop of yogurt or sour cream, or simply with warm crusty bread.

Alternatively, the braise may be left to cool completely and then covered tightly. It will last well in the fridge for up to 3 days. To reheat, spoon into a wide saucepan, add a splash of stock or water if needed, and cover with a lid. Place over a medium heat and bring to a gentle simmer for 5–10 minutes. When piping hot, finish with the herbs and serve as above.

Winter slaw with red cabbage, parsnip & pomegranate

SERVES 4

½ small red cabbage, white centre removed

1 small bulb fennel

2 sticks celery

1 medium parsnip, peeled

2 apples, such as Russet or Cox

1 lemon, juice

1tbsp dried cranberries or sultanas

1tbsp pumpkin seeds

1 small pomegranate

1 bunch watercress, stalks removed, washed and spun dry

FOR THE DRESSING

1tsp Dijon mustard

1tsp honey

4tbsp olive oil

1tbsp sour cream

Slice the cabbage as fine as possible and place in a bowl. Slice the fennel across into rings as thin as possible and slice the celery finely on the angle. Peel the parsnip into ribbons with a vegetable peeler. Grate the apples on a wide grater, including the skin.

Mix all these ingredients with the lemon juice and a little sea salt and freshly ground pepper until well combined. Add the cranberries or sultanas and the pumpkin seeds.

Whisk the dressing ingredients together with some salt and pepper until smooth and pour all over the vegetables. Mix well so that the salad ingredients are thoroughly coated. If necessary, you can leave the salad tightly covered in the fridge for 1–2 hours.

Cut the pomegranate in half around the equator. Holding each half over a bowl, knock the shell with a rolling pin so that the seeds drop out into the bowl. Remove the white membrane, if any, and keep the juices with the seeds on one side, covered.

Just before serving, toss the salad again, then tip out into a serving dish. Garnish with the watercress leaves and scatter the pomegranate seeds and juice over the top.

Savoury tart filled with leek & field mushrooms

The making of pastry is almost unfathomable to the beginner, but once the basics have been mastered, it can be a most useful skill to be used both in savoury and sweet recipes. You will need a tart tin, preferably a fluted one, with a removable base, around 20–22cm in diameter, and approximately 250g of cheap dried beans, which will be used as baking beans. The beans may be used again and again – once cooled, store them in a container with a close-fitting lid.

It is best to first attempt this in a cool kitchen, when you have time to focus, and time to allow the dough to chill in between stages. Alternatively, most supermarkets sell acceptable puff and both sweet and savoury shortcrust pastry ready to roll, but this can be an expensive option.

SERVES 4–8

FOR THE PASTRY
200g plain flour, plus extra
  for dusting
100g butter, cubed
65–75ml chilled water

FOR THE FILLING
50ml olive oil
25g butter
1 large onion, peeled, or 1 large
  leek, trimmed top and root end,
  outer layer removed, cut in half
  lengthwise, washed very well,
  sliced

2 large field mushrooms, peeled
  and finely sliced
100g grated cheese of your choice,
  Cheddar, Swiss-style, Lancashire or
  similar strong hard cheese

FOR THE CUSTARD
2 eggs
100ml double cream
150ml milk
1tsp finely chopped thyme, sage
  or rosemary, or a good pinch
  dried herbs

First, make the pastry. Place the flour in a large bowl with a pinch of sea salt and then the butter in small cubes. Using cool, clean hands, dip your fingers into the bowl and rub the butter into the flour using your fingertips, lifting up the mixture each time and letting it fall back into the bowl. Keep on with this action, digging deep into the bowl, making sure that all the flour gets rubbed in. After a few minutes, the mixture should look like soft white breadcrumbs.

Next, using a fork, add the chilled water little by little, pulling the mixture together to create a ball of dough. Using your hands, gently knead the dough in the bowl, adding a sprinkling of water if it seems too dry, or a little extra flour if it is sticky. Continue kneading until the dough is smooth-ish – remembering that over-handling the dough will result in tough, chewy pastry. Wrap the dough in clingfilm and chill for at least 1 hour or overnight.

Sprinkle a little flour on a clean worktop and, using a rolling pin (or straight-sided wine bottle), roll the dough into a disc approximately 24cm in diameter. If the pastry starts to crumble, push the dough back together gently and start again. If it is sticky, sprinkle the dough, the rolling pin and the table with a little extra flour.

Using the rolling pin or bottle, lift the pastry carefully into the tart tin, lifting up the edges and pushing the dough gently but firmly into the corners and up into the fluted edges of the tin. If holes appear in the dough, use a little of the excess to patch them, pressing them gently over the cracks.

Place the prepared tart shell in the fridge and chill for at least 30 minutes. With a small knife or scissors, trim the excess pastry from around the edges. (Save the trimmings in case you need to patch up any holes later).

Heat the oven to 190°C/fan oven 170°C/mark 5. Cut a disc of baking or greaseproof paper to approximately 4cm wider than the diameter of the tin. Press this into the tart tin, over the pastry, making sure that it is pressed well into the edges. Now fill the pastry-covered paper with the baking beans, again making sure that they fill the corners well. Bake the tart for 25–30 minutes or until the pastry sides are firm and golden brown. Remove the tart from the oven, carefully remove the paper and beans, and check for breakages or damage. If there is a crack or hole, fill it with a little of the saved pastry trimmings.

Place the empty pastry case back in the oven to cook for 5–10 minutes, or until the base is firm and golden brown, then remove from the oven and leave to cool.

Meanwhile, prepare the filling ingredients. In a heavy-based frying pan, heat half the olive oil and half the butter until gently foaming, add the sliced onion or leek and sauté over a medium to high heat, stirring and shaking the pan occasionally, making sure that the slices soften as they turn pale golden at the edges. Add a little extra olive oil if the pan looks dry. Remove to a bowl using a slotted spoon.

Add the remaining olive oil and butter to the pan and cook the mushrooms until they are limp and the juices just start to run. Remove to a separate bowl, as before. At this stage, your tart and all the filling ingredients may be left overnight.

To make the custard, mix together the eggs, cream and milk with some salt and pepper using a whisk until smooth.

To fill the tart, place the tart tin on a baking sheet. Scatter the leek slices over the base, leaving any residual juices in the bowl. Next, place the mushroom slices over the base, minus the juices, followed by the cheese.

Very carefully pour the egg custard over and around the filling ingredients, until it almost reaches the pastry top. Sprinkle with the herbs and gently place in the oven. If the custard spills over the edge, the pastry may stick to the tin and the tart will lose its clean, finished appearance.

Bake for 30–35 minutes or until the custard is puffed and golden. To test the doneness, pierce the egg filling in the centre with a small sharp knife. If the custard runs out liquid, place the tart back in the oven for a few more minutes until it is set.

Remove from the oven and serve immediately, or warm for a few minutes later with a little steamed cavolo nero or savoy cabbage. Alternatively, leave the tart to cool completely and slice the following day for a picnic or a snack on the run.

Mid-afternoon break... high tea

High tea is rather a cosy meal – gloriously old-fashioned.
Perhaps for children just in from school or for a ravenous grown-up
who has somehow managed to miss lunch. It also has the ability
to boost energy levels at the desks of hardworking students,
raise the sugar level of grumpy teens and for those who prefer
not to eat 'too close to bedtime', some of these recipes
could be the perfect answer.

Spring and Summer

Fresh lemonade
Oatmeal, sultana and maple syrup cookies
Egg mayonnaise with anchovy soldiers
Rhubarb and Bramley apple muffins
Brown sugar meringues

Autumn and Winter

Mushrooms on toast with chives and Swiss cheese
Cheddar, anchovy and rosemary scones with black pepper
Fish thumbs
Banana, chocolate, pecan and cinnamon loaf

Fresh lemonade

MAKES 4–8 GLASSES, DEPENDING ON SIZE
80g caster sugar
700ml water
Small handful mint, rosemary or lemon verbena leaves
3 large lemons, juice
1 large orange, juice

First make the sugar syrup. Place the sugar and water in a small pan, bring to the boil and add a small handful of leaves of your choice. Set aside to infuse as it cools.

Mix the lemon and orange juices together in a jug. Pour in the sugar syrup, including the leaves, add ice and serve in tall glasses.

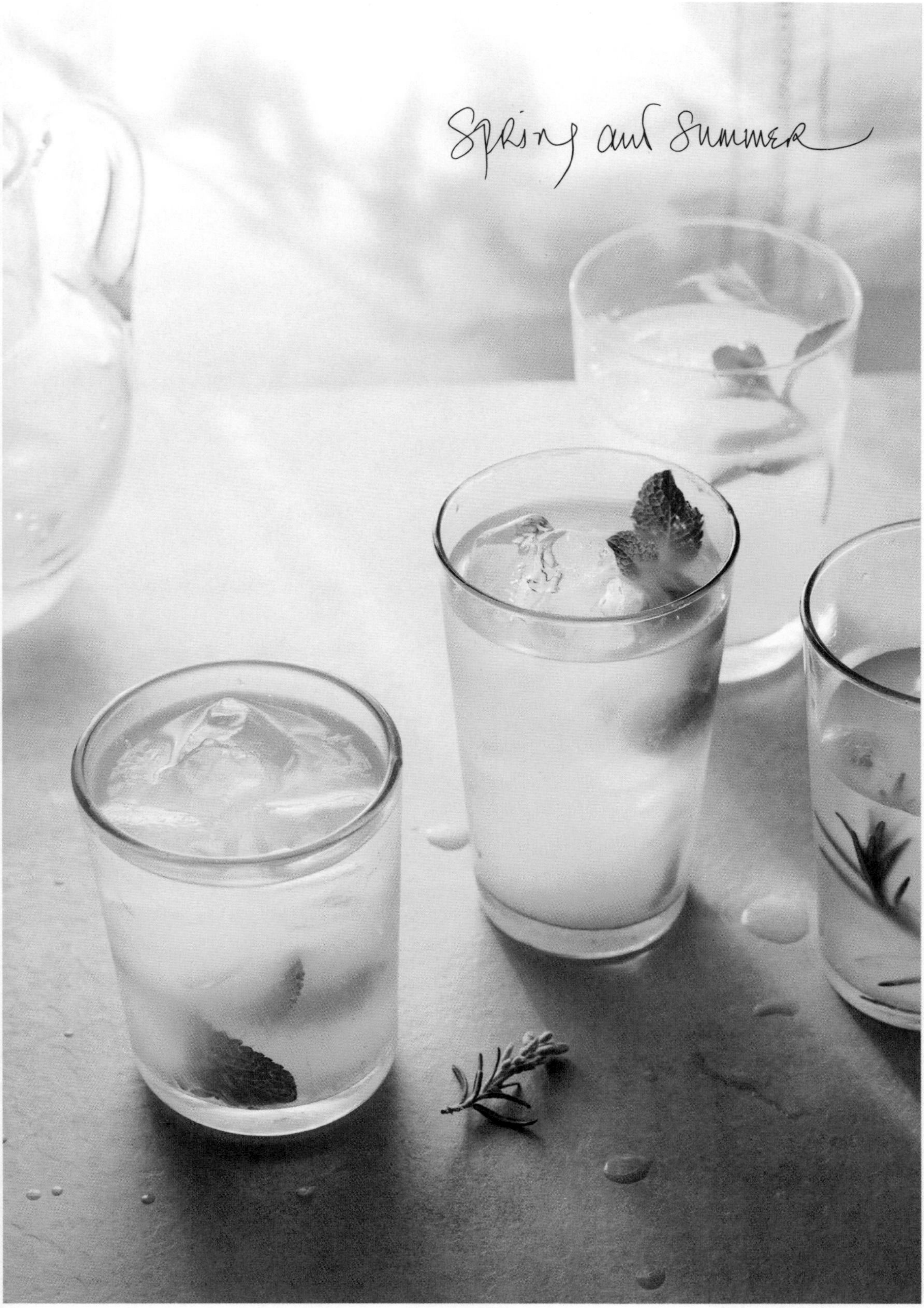
Spring and Summer

Oatmeal, sultana & maple syrup cookies

MAKES 12–14
100g butter, softened
100g soft brown or demerara sugar
100g oatmeal
70g plain flour
Level ½tsp baking powder
75g sultanas
Pinch sea salt
1tbsp maple syrup

Beat the butter and sugar together in a bowl with a wooden spoon until pale, approximately 3 minutes. Add the oatmeal, flour, baking powder, sultanas and sea salt and mix together, either with the wooden spoon or by hand until well blended.

Finally add the maple syrup and mix until everything comes together in a ball and all the sultanas are evenly distributed. Form into a sausage shape approximately 3cm across. Wrap in clingfilm or greaseproof paper and chill for up to 1 hour.

Heat the oven to 170°C/fan oven 150°C/mark 3. Line a baking sheet with baking parchment or greaseproof paper.

Take the cookie dough out of the fridge and cut the roll into 12–14 slices. Place these cut side up on the baking sheet, spaced well apart as they will spread a little on cooking. Alternatively, roll each slice roughly into a ball. Space the balls on the baking sheet, then push each one down gently to slightly flatten them.

Bake for 10–12 minutes, turning the tray halfway through to allow even cooking. When baked, the cookies will be golden brown and crisp at the edges and deliciously chewy on the inside. Cool and store in an airtight container for up to 2 weeks.

Egg mayonnaise with anchovy soldiers

SERVES 2–4 DEPENDING ON APPETITE
4 large free-range or organic eggs
75g butter, softened
4 anchovy fillets, chopped very fine
Approximately 4tbsp mayonnaise (see page 79)
1 tsp lemon juice
4 slices wholemeal or similar bread
Paprika or chilli flakes
A few sprigs watercress, stalks removed, washed and spun dry

Using a large spoon, lower the eggs carefully into a small pan of boiling water and cook for 6 minutes. Drain and leave the eggs in the pan to chill as quickly as possible, under a slowly running cold tap. Once cold, peel the eggs and cut in half, then arrange them cut side down on a serving dish.

Using a wooden spoon or a fork, beat the butter in a small bowl with the chopped anchovy, sea salt and freshly ground pepper until well blended. Leave on one side.

Make the mayonnaise, add the lemon juice and a splash of water to create a pouring consistency and taste for seasoning.

When ready to serve, toast the bread slices on both sides, spread with the anchovy butter and cut into 'soldiers'.

Carefully spoon the mayonnaise over the egg surfaces, one by one, 'masking' the eggs neatly. Sprinkle each one with paprika or chilli flakes and serve immediately, garnished with watercress, with the 'soldiers' on the side.

Rhubarb and Bramley apple muffins

MAKES 10–12

50g butter, melted, plus a little
  extra for greasing the moulds
1 large Bramley apple
1 small stick spring rhubarb
1 orange, finely grated zest and juice
1tsp cinnamon

75g white or brown sugar
1tbsp sour cream
1 large free-range or organic egg
150g plain flour
2tsp baking powder
Pinch sea salt
Icing sugar, for dusting

Using some kitchen towel, wipe a little extra melted butter around the insides of a muffin tin or dishes. This will prevent the muffins from sticking. Alternatively, if you are good at origami, make 12 little 'cups' using squares of greaseproof paper and place them in the holes of the muffin tin or pack them together tightly in an ovenproof dish.

Peel and dice the apple into small hazelnut-sized pieces. Slice the rhubarb into similar sized pieces. The shape does not matter, as they will soften during cooking, but they should be as evenly sized as possible. Mix the apple and rhubarb with the orange zest, juice and cinnamon. Set aside.

Heat the oven to 200°C/fan oven 180°C/mark 6.

Using an electric whisk or mixer, whisk the 50g melted butter with the sugar, sour cream and egg until pale and fluffy. Alternatively, this may be done by hand with a large bowl and whisk, but this will take a little more time and effort. In a separate bowl, mix the flour, baking powder and a pinch of salt and pass through a fine sieve if you have one. Pour the liquids into the flour and mix lightly together, as quickly but as carefully as possible.

Finally, add the fruit, folding all together quickly and gently until blended. Do not over mix, as this may result in heavy, dense muffins.

Using a teaspoon, fill the muffin tin, ramekins or paper cups with the muffin mix – each one should be three quarters full. Bake immediately for 20–25 minutes or until puffed and golden. Leave to cool a little before dusting with icing sugar. Serve with coffee or tea.

Brown sugar meringues

MAKES 8–10 SMALL MERINGUES OR 1 LARGE PAVLOVA
2 egg whites
Pinch salt
80g caster sugar
45g brown sugar
1–2 drops vanilla essence (if you have)

Heat the oven to 140°C/fan oven 120°C/mark 1. Line a baking sheet with a piece of parchment paper.

Using an electric whisk or mixer, whisk the whites with the salt until they are stiff enough to hold their pointed shape at the end of the whisk. Alternatively, this may be done by hand with a large bowl and whisk, but this will take a little more time and effort. Add the caster sugar and continue to whisk for a minute or two, until the meringue is glossy and very stiff. Fold in the brown sugar carefully and add the vanilla.

Scoop the mixture on to the lined baking sheet – perhaps make lots of mini meringues using a teaspoon, or a few larger ones using a tablespoon. Alternatively, you could make one large pavlova-style meringue by pouring the entire contents into one pillowy pile in the centre of the baking sheet, spreading it out a little with the back of a large spoon. Place the meringue/s in the oven and bake as follows:

25–30 minutes for mini meringues; 40 minutes for the larger size; 1 hour for the pavlova. (NB for the pavolva, reduce the oven temperature to 130°C/fan oven 110°C/mark 1 after 30 minutes.)

I like meringue to be crisp on the outside and soft and marshmallowy on the inside, others may prefer a dry, crisp finish. Remove from the oven and set aside to cool.

Serve with ice cream, rhubarb or strawberries in the spring, berries in the summer, poached plums or figs in the autumn, or bananas, pineapple, blood orange or passion fruit in the winter.

Mushrooms on toast with chives & Swiss cheese

This would be a perfect high tea or supper dish, served alongside roasted tomato soup or any other vegetable soup – warming, filling and delicious. Use a cheese that will melt and turn stringy when heated.

SERVES 4

4 large field mushrooms, approximately 400g
50g butter
60ml olive oil
4 thick slices good brown or granary bread (see page 39)
120g grated Swiss or mountain cheese, such as Gruyère, Comté or Raclette, or try Ogleshield from Somerset
1tbsp finely chopped chives
1 bunch watercress, stalks removed, washed and spun dry
Mustard and/or mayonnaise, to serve

Turn on the overhead grill. While it is heating up, peel and slice the mushrooms thinly. Heat the butter and olive oil in a shallow pan, add the mushrooms and cook over a high heat until they have wilted and started to colour a little. Add sea salt and freshly ground pepper and remove from the heat.

Grill the bread on one side until pale golden, then turn over and repeat. Remove from the heat, pile the mushrooms on top and scatter with the grated cheese. Return to the grill and cook until the cheese has melted.

Remove to a chopping board, cut each one in half, then place on individual plates. Sprinkle with chives and serve with watercress or other salad leaves and a dollop of mustard or mayonnaise or both on the side.

Autumn and Winter

Cheddar, anchovy & rosemary scones with black pepper

SERVES 6–10

100g roughly grated mature Chedddar cheese

100g finely grated Parmesan cheese

450g plain flour, plus extra for dusting

30g baking powder

1tsp sea salt

½tsp freshly ground pepper

100g butter, cubed

500g buttermilk or plain yogurt

½tsp very finely chopped rosemary, plus a few sprigs to garnish

6–8 anchovy fillets, finely chopped (optional)

A little milk, for brushing

Heat the oven to 180°C/fan oven 160°C/mark 4 and line a baking sheet with baking parchment.

Place the first 4 ingredients in a large bowl with the salt and pepper and mix. Rub butter into the dry ingredients until the mixture resembles medium crumbs.

Add the buttermilk or yogurt, rosemary and the anchovy fillets, if using, then mix with a fork until everything comes together. Very gently knead the dough together in the bowl, then tip it out onto a lightly floured board. Shape into a flat disc, approximately 30cm across and 4cm thick.

Place the disc of dough onto the lined baking sheet, then brush all over with the milk. Using the long handle of a wooden spoon, create a criss-cross of indentations over the top to mark out 8 or 10 triangles, pressing down no more than half the way into the dough. Garnish each portion with the rosemary sprigs and sprinkle with sea salt.

Bake for 35-45 minutes or until puffed and golden, turning halfway through the cooking time for even baking.

Serve as soon as possible, broken along the indentations with lots of butter, or as an accompaniment to a vegetable soup or a salad.

This will last for at least 3 days in an airtight container.

Fish thumbs

Possibly the most classic of high tea treats – and one I remember rather fondly.

The fish fingers of my childhood were no doubt bought-in and ready made, then my mother would shallow-fry them in vegetable oil until crisp and golden, and serve to my brothers and me after a fun-filled day at school, followed by a long walk home.

As youngsters, we were not allowed access to a television until the weekend as homework always took precedent. But sitting around the table bickering or trying to out-do each other was part of the game before bedtime. How my mother kept her cool until my father arrived home in the evening remains a mystery!

As with all things fish-related, the freshness of the product is paramount. I am blessed in knowing a rather special part of North Cornwall, near Port Isaac, including some of the local fishermen and the shops, cafes and restaurants that work with them.

A week there in the summer sun (or wind and torrential rain!) is all I need to recharge the batteries after a long, hard, busy winter. At the restaurant, we are equally blessed with suppliers who source their fish directly from boats in the West Country.

Whilst not everyone has direct access to a community such as this, getting to know your local fishmonger is vital if you wish to enjoy the very best produce of the sea. For this recipe, choose a firm white fish such a cod, haddock or pollock and make doubly sure that the bones are removed along with the skin. If you are uncomfortable doing this, your fishmonger will do it for you – but always double check their work when you get home by running a finger along the side of the fillet, to check for any stray bones.

SERVES 3–4
500g fillets of firm white fish, eg cod, haddock or pollock
50g flour, well seasoned with salt and pepper
1 large free-range or organic egg, whisked with salt,
  pepper and a little milk
125g dried breadcrumbs (see page 152)
Vegetable oil, for frying

TO SERVE
Lemon mayonnaise (see page 79)
Lemon wedges

Firstly, line a baking sheet with baking paper.

Cut the fillets into small thumb-sized pieces. It is important that they are as equally sized as possible as they need to cook evenly.

Prepare 3 bowls with the dipping ingredients: the seasoned flour, whisked egg and breadcrumbs. One by one, dip the fish pieces into the flour, gently knock off the excess and lay on a board. Next, using one hand, dip the pieces into the egg one by one, lifting out to drain, then place into the bowl of crumbs. Using the 'dry hand', coat the pieces in the crumbs on all sides. One by one, repeat the process, leaving the crumbed fillets on the paper-lined baking sheet.

Once they are all coated, they may be left, covered, in the fridge for a few hours before cooking.

Preheat the oven to 170°C/fan oven 150°C/mark 3 and prepare a baking sheet lined with some kitchen paper.

Heat a shallow non-stick pan with enough oil to just cover the surface. Test the heat by sprinkling a few breadcrumbs into the pan. As soon as they sizzle gently, the oil is hot enough to use. Carefully lay the fillets into the pan, a few at a time, and cook until golden brown on one side. Turn over gently (they will be fragile) and cook the other side, about 2–3 minutes in total, depending on the thickness of the fillets.

Remove to the prepared baking sheet and keep warm in the oven while frying the remaining fillets. Sprinkle with sea salt and serve on warm plates with the mayonnaise, lemon wedges and a steamed green vegetable.

Banana, chocolate, pecan & cinnamon loaf

SERVES 6–8

2 free-range or organic eggs
125ml vegetable oil, plus extra
  for greasing
200g sugar
3 small bananas
125g dark chocolate, finely chopped

140g self-raising flour
1tsp baking powder
1tsp cinnamon
Pinch salt
85g chopped pecans, or other
  nuts of your choice

Using a piece of kitchen towel, wipe a loaf tin or dish with a splash of vegetable oil. Line with 2 long, wide strips of greaseproof paper, making a criss-cross across the base and pushing them into the corners and up the sides. Wipe the paper with a little oil. This will prevent the loaf from sticking while it is cooking.

Using an electric whisk or mixer, whisk the eggs, 125ml oil and the sugar until thick. Alternatively, this may be done by hand using a large bowl and a whisk, but this will take a little more time and effort. Chop 2½ of the bananas finely and add to the egg mixture with the chocolate.

In a separate bowl, mix the flour, baking powder, cinnamon and salt and add the pecans. Pour the liquids into the flour mixture and stir together carefully but thoroughly.

Heat the oven to 180°C/fan oven 160°C/mark 4. Scrape the mix into the container carefully, then slice the remaining ½ banana and arrange the slices decoratively on top. Bake on the middle shelf for 40–50 minutes.

To test if the loaf is cooked, push a sharp knife or skewer into the centre. When it is removed, it should be hot but dry. If the mixture has stuck to it, it means that it is still partially raw, so will need a few more minutes.

Once baked, remove from the oven and leave to cool slightly, then gently pull the ends of the greaseproof paper strips up and away from the tin to release the loaf. Allow to cool completely before slicing and serving.

Supper... to fill a gap

Sometimes we simply do not want 'big' food,
but we nevertheless want it to feel special. There is often talk
of the 'comfort' of food and how we as humans gain a sense of
nurturing through what we eat, but guilt should not be part of this!
Whilst the following recipes may take a little time to assemble,
comfort may also be received through that process of preparation,
so it should seem worth the effort.

Spring and Summer

Fish soup with rice and fennel

Baked cheese in a box

Fish cakes

Savoury bread and butter pudding with cheese and herbs

Autumn and Winter

Baked onion soup with Gruyère toasts

Cod and smoked haddock pie with leeks, mushrooms, parsley and potato

Steamed mussels with cream, parsley and spring onions

Bramley apples filled with cinnamon, brown sugar, pecans and sultanas

Spring and Summer

Fish soup with rice & fennel

Very often fishmongers will simply throw away the fish bones
once the fillets have been sold, as sadly few customers want them,
or know what to do with them. However, the bones can be made
into a valuable, tasty and nutritious soup or stock, with just a few
vegetables, herbs and 45 minutes of your time. Check that the bones
are fresh and, if it is a sunny day, ask the fishmonger to put them in
a bag with some ice so that they stay cool as you travel home.

SERVES 4–8, DEPENDING ON WHETHER SERVING AS A MAIN MEAL OR AS A STARTER

FOR THE BROTH

Approximately 1kg fresh fish bones,
   ideally from white fish such as brill,
   cod, haddock, plaice or sole
1 large onion, peeled and roughly
   chopped
2 sticks celery, roughly chopped
1 bulb fennel, roughly chopped

1 small leek, well rinsed
3 bay leaves
A few sprigs thyme, parsley and
   rosemary
A few peppercorns
1 large clove garlic, peeled and
   crushed

First make the broth. Rinse the fish bones under a cold running tap. Cut
or break the bones into pieces that will easily fit into a medium-sized
saucepan. Place them in the pan, cover with cold water and leave on one
side while you prepare the vegetables.

Place all the vegetables on top of the fish bones and add the herbs,
peppercorns and garlic. Bring slowly to the boil over a medium heat.
Using a ladle or spoon, skim the foam away as it rises to the surface and
discard. Simmer gently for 20–30 minutes or until the broth is flavourful.

Remove from the heat and strain the broth through a fine sieve into a
clean pan. This may now be cooled and kept in the fridge, covered, for
up to 3 days and used as fish stock for a risotto (see page 107) or pasta
dish. It will normally become slightly 'jellied' on cooling.

FOR THE SOUP

150g long-grain, arborio, brown or basmati rice
1 bulb fennel, sliced into rings or chopped medium-fine
400g fish fillets, such as cod, haddock, brill, pollock, whiting or hake
3tbsp olive oil
2tbsp chopped parsley
2tbsp chopped celery leaves
Chives or spring onion, finely sliced
A few spinach leaves, stalks removed, washed and torn or
  roughly sliced
150ml double cream (optional)
Crusty bread, to serve

To make the soup, measure approximately 1.2 litres of broth into a clean pan, add the rice and fennel and bring gently to a boil. Turn the heat down to a simmer for 7–10 minutes while you prepare the remaining ingredients.

Cut the pieces of fish into small slices and place in a bowl. Add the olive oil, chopped herbs, chives or spring onion and a little sea salt and freshly ground pepper.

Taste the rice after 7–10 minutes and when almost cooked, add the fish mixture and continue to cook gently for 2–3 minutes or until the rice is tender and the fish is flaking. Taste and add salt if necessary. Lastly, add the spinach leaves, giving it one final stir as too much movement will break up the flakes of fish.

For a richer version of this soup, add 150ml double cream with the spinach, or if a more robust soup is required (to serve as a main meal perhaps), a selection of other vegetables could be added to the fennel and rice, for example sliced onion, mushrooms, carrot and celery.

Ladle the soup carefully into warm soup bowls and serve with chunks of crusty bread.

Baked cheese in a box

Perhaps the quickest and most satisfying of ways to feed 2 or
3 hungry people when there is still a slight nip in the spring air – is
this gloriously rich but more-ish dish. Quick and simple to prepare,
when placed in the centre of a table it can bring friends and family
together in the most delicious way!

SERVES 2, 3 OR EVEN 4
1 'boxed' cheese of your choice – ideally Baron Bigod, Tunworth,
   Camembert or Vacherin
1 large clove garlic, centre shoot removed if present
Rosemary sprigs
¼–½ loaf bread of your choice
Good olive oil
Runny honey (optional)

Heat the oven to 180°C/fan oven 160°C/mark 4.

Unwrap the cheese (if in paper) and return to the balsa wood box. With
a small, sharp knife, pierce the top skin of the cheese in 10 or 12 evenly
spaced places. Slice the garlic finely and gently push a slice, along with
a small sprig of rosemary, into each hole. Place the cheese (in its box)
into an ovenproof serving dish and bake for 5 minutes or until the tips of
garlic and rosemary start to colour.

Meanwhile, slice the bread into 8 or 10 chunks or slices for dipping.
Remove the dish from the oven and place the bread around the outside
of the cheese. Drizzle them with a little olive oil and sprinkle with sea
salt. Return the dish to the oven for a further 8–10 minutes or until the
toasts are golden at the edges and the cheese has just started to ooze from
the side.

Serve immediately on warm plates, drizzled with honey if you like, and
using the breads to dip into the molten cheese.

Fish cakes

SERVES 4

350g large potatoes, peeled and cut into large even-sized chunks
2 bay leaves
450g fish fillets, such as cod, haddock, hake or salmon, or a mixture
  of 2 or 3
2tbsp chopped herbs, such as dill, parsley, chives or celery leaf
½ lemon, grated zest
2 large free-range or organic eggs
1tbsp double cream (optional)
4tbsp plain flour
6–8tbsp dried breadcrumbs (see following page)
4tbsp vegetable oil
50g butter
Tartare sauce or garlic mayonnaise (see page 82) or tomato
  ketchup, to serve

Cook the potatoes with the bay leaves in a saucepan of boiling salted
water. When the potatoes are tender, drain and keep on one side,
retaining the water. Using a potato masher, mash the potatoes until fluffy
and lump-free, then set aside.

Remove any bones from the fish using tweezers, then place the fillets in
a medium-sized pan. Cover with the warm potato water and cook gently
over a medium heat for 510 minutes or until the fish flakes easily apart
with a fork. Drain and leave to cool, discarding the liquid.

Place the mashed potato and fish in a bowl and mix together with a fork,
breaking up the fish until evenly distributed. Season with sea salt and
freshly ground pepper and add the herbs, lemon zest, 1 lightly beaten egg
and the cream (if using).

Taste the mixture for seasoning, then shape by hand into 4 smooth
even-sized patties, approximately 2.5cm thick. These may now be left,
covered, in the fridge for up to 3 days. »

When you are ready to fry the fish cakes, prepare 3 bowls: the 4tbsp flour, seasoned generously with salt and pepper; the remaining egg, whisked with a splash of cold water; and the 6–8tbsp dried breadcrumbs.

First roll the fish cakes in the flour, brushing off the excess. Lay them one by one on a clean work surface. Next, using one hand only, dip the fish cakes, one by one into the egg, rolling them carefully around, coating the surfaces and allowing the excess egg to drip back into the bowl. Place the coated fishcakes on a large plate. With clean, dry hands, dip the wet fish cakes into the breadcrumbs, pressing the crumbs gently into the egg. Reshape as necessary, making them smooth and even in thickness.

In a heavy-based frying pan, heat the oil and butter until foaming. Fry the fish cakes until golden and crisp on one side, flip over carefully with a fish slice or palette knife and fry on the other side until golden. Cook through for up to 5 minutes on each side and drain on kitchen paper. Keep warm in a low oven and serve within 30 minutes with tartare sauce, garlic mayonnaise or ketchup.

To make dried breadcrumbs

½ loaf of 2 or 3-day-old bread – ideally plain white or sourdough

Remove most of the crust from the old bread, then cut into even sized pieces, the smaller the better. Place on a baking sheet in the oven. Turn the temperature to 130°C/fan oven 110°C/mark 1 and bake until dry, approximately 1–1½ hours.

Place the bread in a sealed bag or wrapped in a clean tea towel and lay on a table, holding the opening tightly shut. Using a rolling pin or the underside of a small pan, bash the bag of dried bread until it all becomes crumbs. Leave to cool, then simply place into an airtight container and use within 2 weeks. (The crumbs will last up to 3 months in the freezer.)

Savoury bread & butter pudding with cheese & herbs

SERVES 4–6
12–14 thin slices baguette or wholemeal bread
30g butter
2tsp chopped thyme or 1tsp chopped dried herbs
100g grated Cheddar cheese
4 free-range or organic eggs
50ml milk
Salad or crudités, to serve

Spread the bread slices with butter on one side.

In an ovenproof dish with a capacity of approximately 1.2 litres, lay the bread slices neatly overlapping one another, and sprinkle with half the chopped herbs and half the grated cheese.

Whisk the eggs with the milk and some sea salt and freshly ground pepper until smooth and frothy. Carefully pour the egg mixture into the dish, making sure that the slices are evenly covered. Scatter the remaining herbs and cheese over and leave to soak for 10–20 minutes.

Heat the oven to 180°C/fan oven 160°C/mark 4. After 10–20 minutes soaking time, place the dish in the oven and bake for 20–25 minutes or until the egg has puffed and the bread has turned golden brown all over. Pierce the centre with a sharp knife and if the egg runs liquid, place the dish back into the oven for a few more minutes. If the egg starts to colour before it is cooked in the centre, cover loosely with aluminium foil to continue the cooking without burning the top.

Serve as soon as possible with a salad of various leaves or raw vegetable crudités of celery, fennel, carrot or radishes, for example. Leftovers may be chilled overnight in the fridge, then sliced like a cake for a lovely picnic or lunch-on-the-run idea.

Baked onion soup with Gruyère toasts

This is such a rich and filling dish, especially if a deeply flavoured meat stock has been used, that very little is required either before or after it. Perhaps a lovely selection of raw vegetable crudités beforehand or a crisp bitter leaf salad with or after would be all that is needed. Either way, a bottle of full-bodied red wine is the perfect accompaniment.

SERVES 6

6 medium–large onions (approximately 750g)
90g butter
6 bay leaves
1tsp chopped rosemary or thyme
¼ bottle good red wine
1 litre good stock – beef, chicken or vegetable
½ baguette or sourdough loaf
Olive oil, for drizzling
250g Gruyère cheese

Peel the onions, then slice them as finely as possible, following the instructions on page 22.

Melt the butter in a large heavy-based pan over a medium to high heat, then add the onions little by little, stirring them well so that the slices become coated in the butter as they start to cook.

Once the onions are all in, add the bay leaves and the chopped herbs. Cook, stirring from time to time, so that the onions brown evenly and do not get caught at the bottom of the pan. After 15–20 minutes, the onion juices will start to flow and the volume of onions will have reduced by at least 50 per cent. »

When the onion slices are all a lovely chestnut brown, add the red wine and season with sea salt and pepper. Stir everything together well, making sure that the soup is evenly coloured throughout and the texture of the onion is very soft. (This is not a place for al dente onion!) Simmer for 2–3 minutes and reduce the liquid by approximately a half.

Add the stock and stir again to mix well, bring to the boil, then simmer for up to 30 minutes or until the flavour and the smell is pleasing. At this stage the soup may be removed from the heat and left to cool, then stored, well covered, in the fridge for up to 3 days. Alternatively, it may be frozen.

Before serving, heat the oven to 180°C/fan oven 160°C/mark 4. If the soup has been chilled, heat it in a large pan until gently simmering.

Slice the bread into evenly sized pieces (ideally 2 per person) and grate the Gruyère. Lay the bread on a baking sheet, drizzle with olive oil and bake for 3–4 minutes or until golden on one side. Remove from the oven.

Pour the onion soup into an ovenproof serving bowl or deep dish and place the toasts, un-toasted sides up, over the top, slightly overlapping each other. Scatter the toasts with the grated cheese and place the dish in the oven to bake for 10–15 minutes, until the cheese has melted and the toasts are crisp at the edges.

To serve, scoop into warm serving bowls and then ladle the juices in over the top. Each guest should have an equal quantity of sliced onions, juice and toasts.

Cod & smoked haddock pie with leeks, mushrooms, parsley & potato

SERVES 4–5

300g cod, haddock or pollock fillet, bones removed with tweezers
250g smoked haddock fillet, bones removed with tweezers
400ml milk
250ml water
3 bay leaves
1–2 sprigs thyme, sage or rosemary
Pinch sea salt and freshly ground pepper
1 medium leek, trimmed top and root end, outer layer removed
2 large field mushrooms, peeled
50g butter
2–4tbsp olive oil
50g plain flour
2tbsp roughly chopped parsley

FOR THE POTATOES

1kg potatoes, peeled and cut into walnut-sized pieces
60ml milk, warmed in a small pan
20g butter

Place the fish fillets into a medium-sized pan, cover with the milk and water, then add the bay leaves, thyme, sea salt and pepper. Bring to a simmer. Cover and continue to cook very gently for 5–7 minutes or until the fish flakes easily apart when pierced with a small knife. Leave on one side to cool.

Cut the leek in half lengthwise, wash carefully to remove any grit within, then cut across into ½cm slices. Slice the mushrooms thinly.

Place half the butter and half the olive oil in a wide shallow pan and heat until sizzling. Add the leeks and cook over a medium heat until soft, » approximately 3 minutes. Remove with a slotted spoon to a small bowl.

Add the mushrooms to the pan with a little extra olive oil and cook in the same way over a medium to high heat for 2–3 minutes until they have softened, starting to release their juices. Season with salt and pepper. Remove with a slotted spoon as before and mix with the leeks.

Heat the juices in the pan with the remaining butter until sizzling, add the flour and stir over a medium heat until it resembles pale sand. Drain the milky juice from the fish by pouring it through a sieve over a bowl or jug and, little by little, whisk this into the pan over the heat. The sauce will thicken immediately, but continue to whisk until smooth, approximately 2–3 minutes. Taste and adjust the seasoning.

Peel the skin away from the fish and discard. Flake or break the fish into equal-size pieces into an ovenproof dish approximately 1.5 litres in volume. Scatter the leek and mushroom mixture over, and then the chopped parsley. Finally, pour the sauce over to cover evenly. Using a fork, very gently mix the ingredients together a little, without breaking up the fish. Leave to cool.

Meanwhile, prepare the potatoes. Cook in boiling, salted water until tender, drain and then mash with a potato masher or strong whisk until very smooth. Next, stir in the warm milk and butter, then season to taste with salt and pepper.

While still warm, spoon the potato over the fish dish until neatly covered. You may like to finish the top using a fork or table knife by making sweeping shapes in the soft potato. If you are a dab hand with a piping bag, you may like to be even cleverer.

Once cold, the pie can now be covered and left in the fridge for up to 3 days before baking. To bake, heat the oven to 180°C/fan oven 160°C/mark 4.

Place the dish on a baking sheet (in case of spillage during cooking) on the middle shelf of the oven and bake for up to 20–25 minutes or until the sauce has started to bubble around the edges and the potato is crisp and golden.

Serve with steamed shredded cabbage, kale, chard or leaf broccoli.

Steamed mussels with cream, parsley & spring onions

SERVES 2–4
1kg mussels
1 glass white wine
1 small bunch spring onions, finely chopped
250ml double cream
1tbsp chopped parsley
Crusty bread, toasted, to serve

Put the mussels in the sink with lots of cold running water, scrub them well and pull away any remaining beards that may still be attached to the shells. Discard any that may be cracked or refusing to close.

Place the cleaned mussels into a very large saucepan (they will expand on cooking, so make sure they do not fill more than half the pan). Add the wine, a splash of water and the finely chopped spring onions. Put a tight fitting lid on the top and cook over a high heat for 4–5 minutes, shaking the pan or stirring the contents occasionally to allow even cooking.

Once the mussels have all opened, remove them with a slotted spoon to a large warm serving bowl. Place the pan containing the juices back onto the heat and add the cream, then bring to the boil and cook for 1–2 minutes.

Pour this over the mussels – carefully, as there may be a little grit left in the bottom, similar to the sediment in the base of a bottle of old red wine. No matter how carefully you may have scrubbed the molluscs, some shells retain sand within.

Sprinkle the mussels with parsley and serve immediately with crusty toasted bread to soak up the salty juices.

Bramley apples filled with cinnamon, brown sugar, pecans & sultanas

SERVES 4

4 small, evenly sized Bramley apples – these are pale green in colour with
  smooth, slightly oily skins
50g pecan nuts, roughly chopped
50g sultanas
25g brown sugar
4 pinches ground cinnamon
Whipped cream or ice cream, to serve (optional)

Heat the oven to 180°C/fan oven 160°C/mark 4.

Wash the apples and then scoop out the cores. This is best done with an
apple corer, but you can use a teaspoon or small knife instead, burrowing
in from the top to the middle, then from the bottom up to the middle.
The idea is to remove as much of the core as possible without disturbing
the apple around it.

With the tip of a knife, cut through the skin around the equator of each
apple (this will prevent it from bursting in the oven), then place them into
a deep baking or roasting dish, fitting them snugly next to each other.
Divide the pecans and sultanas between the 4 holes, then sprinkle over
the brown sugar and cinnamon.

Pour a splash of boiling water from a kettle around the apples to just
cover the base of the dish. Cover with aluminium foil and bake for
45–50 minutes or until almost tender when pierced with a knife. Remove
the foil and continue to cook until the apples are a little crusty around
the edges, but take care, as the apples easily collapse if over cooked.

Leave to cool a little – to some, these can be even more wonderful served
cold – then serve with whipped cream, ice cream or simply nude.

Supper... to last until breakfast

As a restaurateur, I find keen appetites a joy to observe.
The sight of happy conversation around a table along with the sound
of cutlery on the plate and the chink of glasses is what we strive to
achieve each day. For those at home, having spent time at the stove
and the sink in an apron, to see a child wholeheartedly embracing an
evening meal is surely a parent's joy, and a blessing.

Spring and Summer

Leek and pea soup
Roasted chicken with potatoes, carrots, red onion and watercress
Light chicken stock and risotto

Autumn and Winter

Winter green salad with cauliflower, almonds, currants and mustard
Tomato, mozzarella and basil galette
Rabbit with pappardelle, parsley and Parmesan
Herbed and spiced meatballs
Roasted tomato soup with curly kale and chickpeas

Leek & pea soup

SERVES 4–6
2tbsp olive oil, plus extra for drizzling
25g butter
4 sprigs thyme
2 bay leaves
3 large leeks, trimmed top and root end, outer layer removed,
  washed very well and sliced
1 small onion, peeled and chopped
2 sticks celery, chopped
2 medium potatoes, peeled and chopped
½ bulb fennel, chopped
850ml vegetable or light chicken stock or ½ water/½ stock
120g peas – frozen is fine but fresh is best
2tbsp sour cream or yogurt, to serve

Place the olive oil and butter in a heavy-based medium pan with the thyme and bay leaves. Over a high heat, add the leeks, onion, celery, potatoes and fennel and stir until the vegetables start to soften. Add sea salt and freshly ground pepper and just cover with the stock or water. Bring to a gentle simmer, cover and cook until all is soft (approximately 15–20 minutes). Allow to cool a little before straining some of the juice from the pan – keep this juice for later.

Place the vegetables and remaining juice in a liquidiser and purée until smooth, adding the saved juice to create the correct consistency (similar to thick double cream). Pour through a sieve into a clean pan, pushing the soup through with the back of a ladle. Discard the debris, taste the soup and adjust the seasoning if necessary.

Bring the peas to the boil in a small pan of salted water, cook for 1–2 minutes (if fresh) or 1–2 seconds (if frozen), drain and then season with a splash of extra olive oil, salt and pepper.

Heat the soup and serve garnished with peas and a spoon of cream, yogurt or a drizzle of olive oil. This soup is also wonderful served chilled.

Spring and Summer

Roasted chicken with potatoes, carrots, red onion & watercress

This wonderful chicken will give you 3, maybe even 4 meals. Choose a large generous looking bird and be prepared for lots of leftovers, and lots of different ways in which to use every last little bit of it.

SERVES 4 PLUS LEFTOVERS

FOR THE CHICKEN
1.8kg free-range or organic chicken
1 large white onion, peeled and chopped into 8 wedges
2 large carrots, peeled and roughly chopped
3 sticks celery, roughly chopped
60ml olive oil
1tbsp chopped thyme
2 bunches watercress, to serve

FOR THE POTATOES, CARROTS AND ONIONS
60ml olive oil
50g butter
1tbsp chopped rosemary or 1tsp chopped dried herbs
4 cloves garlic, peeled and sliced
1kg Maris Piper potatoes (or similar roasting potatoes), peeled and cut into even-sized pieces
4 carrots, peeled and halved lengthwise
4 red onions, cut into 4 across the root (I like to keep the skin on)

FOR THE GRAVY
1tbsp plain flour
400ml light chicken or vegetable stock or water

Untie the chicken and remove the bag of giblets, if any. (This will include the neck, gizzard, heart and liver, to be used later.) Pull and stretch the legs and wing tips slightly away from the body. Trim away the wing tips and any excess fatty skin at the neck end. Wipe the cavity with kitchen paper and season well inside with sea salt and freshly ground pepper. Heat the oven to 180°C/fan oven 160°C/mark 4.

Place the white onion, 2 carrots and 3 sticks celery in a roasting tray and lay the chicken on top with the wing tips. Drizzle with olive oil and rub it all over (this is best done by hand), then sprinkle generously with salt, pepper and chopped thyme.

Roast the chicken for 20–30 minutes on the middle shelf of the oven or until the skin has started to turn golden. Halfway through this cooking time, remove the roasting tray from the oven and, using a large spoon, baste the chicken skin with the oils at the bottom of the tray. This will enhance the flavour and texture of the skin. After a further 10 minutes roasting time, take the chicken tray from the oven and, with tongs or a carving fork, turn the chicken over to roast upside down for a further 25–35 minutes or until the thigh juices run clear when pierced with a small sharp knife.

Meanwhile, prepare the potatoes. Combine the olive oil, butter and rosemary in a second ovenproof dish or roasting tin and place on the top shelf of the oven to heat up.

Place the potatoes and carrots in a pan of salted water and bring to a boil, then cook for 2–3 minutes or until just the outside of the potato has started to soften. Drain well, then remove the carrots and set aside. Tip the potatoes carefully into the hot fat in the ovenproof dish or tin, place the potatoes on the top shelf of the oven and roast for up to 30 minutes or until pale golden on all sides. Shake the potatoes and turn them over once or twice during the roasting, to prevent them from sticking to the dish.

Add the carrots and red onion wedges to the potatoes, stirring them together gently to coat in the herby oils. Continue to roast for a further 20 minutes until all are tender inside and crusty on the outside. Remove from the oven and set aside, ready for reheating. Leave the oven on. »

At this stage, the chicken also should be cooked, so remove the roasting tray from the oven and carefully lift the chicken into a large bowl. Cover with a plate or aluminium foil and leave to 'rest' in a warm place.

Meanwhile, wash the watercress carefully in cold water, picking out and discarding the large stalks. Spin or shake dry and place in a bowl and leave in the fridge until ready to serve.

To make the gravy, skim away the excess fat from the juices in the chicken roasting tray and discard. Place the tray on the hob over a low heat, stir in the flour and cook for 2 minutes while stirring. Add the stock or water and bring to a gentle simmer, scraping up all the vegetables that may have stuck to the base of the tray. Taste, season and strain the juices into a small pan through a sieve. Skim away any excess fat if necessary and discard, along with the vegetable debris.

If using, the liver and heart may now be trimmed and rinsed in cold water. Cut them into small dice and add to the gravy, then simmer very gently while the rest of the dish is finished.

Put the potato and carrot dish back into the oven and roast the vegetables for up to 10 minutes or until crisp and piping hot.

Place the chicken on a chopping board and pour the juices from the bowl (if any) into the gravy. Remove the legs and cut into 2 at the joint. Remove the breasts from the carcass and cut each into two or three and place all on a warm serving platter with the roasted vegetables. Alternatively, you may prefer to carve the chicken at the table.

To serve, skim the gravy if necessary and serve alongside the chicken with the roasted vegetables, garnished with the watercress leaves.

What will be left are the remaining giblets, the carcass and perhaps some chicken juices from the chopping board. Depending on the appetites of your supper guests, you may also have some chicken left over too.

After the meal it is important that all elements of the leftovers are kept safely. This means covering them tightly and leaving them in a fridge until the next stage of cooking is embarked upon.

Light chicken stock

1 chicken carcass and the giblets (neck and gizzard)
Few sprigs herbs
2 bay leaves
1 glass red or white wine
A few peppercorns
Approximately 1 teacup full each of roughly chopped onion,
  celery and carrot

Remove all the meat from the leg and wing bones and check the carcass too. (There is a lovely nugget of meat, called the oyster, at either side of the backbone where it meets the thigh joint, which is not to be missed.) Keep this meat well covered in the fridge.

Place all the bones, skin and cartilage in a large pan with the remaining gravy, if any. Rinse the neck and gizzard from the giblet bag and add to the pan. Barely cover with cold water, add the herbs, the red or white wine, a few peppercorns and the vegetables.

Bring to a simmer and cook slowly for up to 1 hour, occasionally skimming away any impurities that may rise to the surface.

Strain the stock through a fine sieve, discard the debris, and cool as quickly as possible, then store in the fridge for up to 3 days. Alternatively, chill the stock in a selection of small containers and freeze them, labelled and dated, for future use, such as in soups, risottos or stews.

So you now have a lovely stock – or indeed a soup, if you prefer. Here is a suggestion for how to use it.

Cook pasta (linguini, penne, orzo for example) in the normal way in boiling salted water until just cooked, then drain. Put back into the pan with some shredded spinach, watercress leaves, grated carrots and/or leftover peas or sweetcorn. Barely cover with the stock, bring to the boil, taste and serve. This is the BEST form of pot noodles!

Make a delicious risotto

600ml chicken stock (see opposite) or fish or vegetable stock
80g butter
4tbsp olive oil
1 onion, peeled and finely diced
250g arborio or carnaroli rice
1tsp chopped thyme, rosemary or sage
1 glass dry white wine
250g total weight of vegetables of your choice – for example, very finely
sliced mushrooms, asparagus or courgette, or peas or fava beans
75g soft goat's cheese, ricotta or grated Parmesan
1tbsp chopped soft herbs, such as parsley, chives, basil or tarragon
Salad, to serve

Gently bring the stock to a simmer in a small pan.

Heat half the butter and all the olive oil in a saucepan and cook the finely
chopped onion over a medium heat, stirring from time to time, until soft,
but not coloured, approximately 2–3 minutes.

Add the arborio or carnaroli rice with a little sea salt, freshly ground
pepper and the thyme, rosemary or sage, and continue to cook until the
oil and butter have been absorbed. Add the wine and cook until it too
has been absorbed.

Gradually stir the warm stock, little by little, into the risotto until
the rice is cooked and the consistency is to your liking. This will take
approximately 15–20 minutes and you need to stir from time to time
to prevent sticking and to make sure the rice is cooked evenly. Halfway
through the addition of the stock, add the vegetables of your choice,
which need only a few minutes' cooking time.

Finally, stir in the remaining butter, cheese of your choice and soft herbs,
then serve in warm bowls with a salad of leaves on the side.

Winter green salad with cauliflower, almonds, currants & mustard

A simple roasted chicken could be served alongside this, or baked potatoes filled with goat's cheese or sour cream.

SERVES 4 AS A SIDE SALAD
150g curly kale or ¼ Savoy cabbage
½ small cauliflower
75g almonds, skin on
6tbsp olive oil
60g currants
2tsp wholegrain or Dijon mustard
½ lemon, juice
½ bunch spring onions, finely sliced

Wash the kale or cabbage, then shred it finely with a sharp knife. As this will be eaten raw, it needs to be cut as finely as you can manage (in order for it to not taste and feel like cattle feed!)

Break the cauliflower into florets (or use a small knife) and blanch in a small pan of boiling salted water for 1–2 minutes. Drain and then slice roughly into bite-sized pieces.

Slice or chop the almonds roughly and place in a small frying pan with the olive oil. Heat gently and toast for a few seconds, stirring occasionally, but take care as these will burn easily. Remove from the heat and pour the toasted nuts and oil into a salad bowl.

Add the currants, mustard and lemon juice to the almonds, season with sea salt and freshly ground pepper, and mix well.

When ready to serve, mix the kale, cauliflower and spring onions into the dressing, toss gently but thoroughly together, and serve.

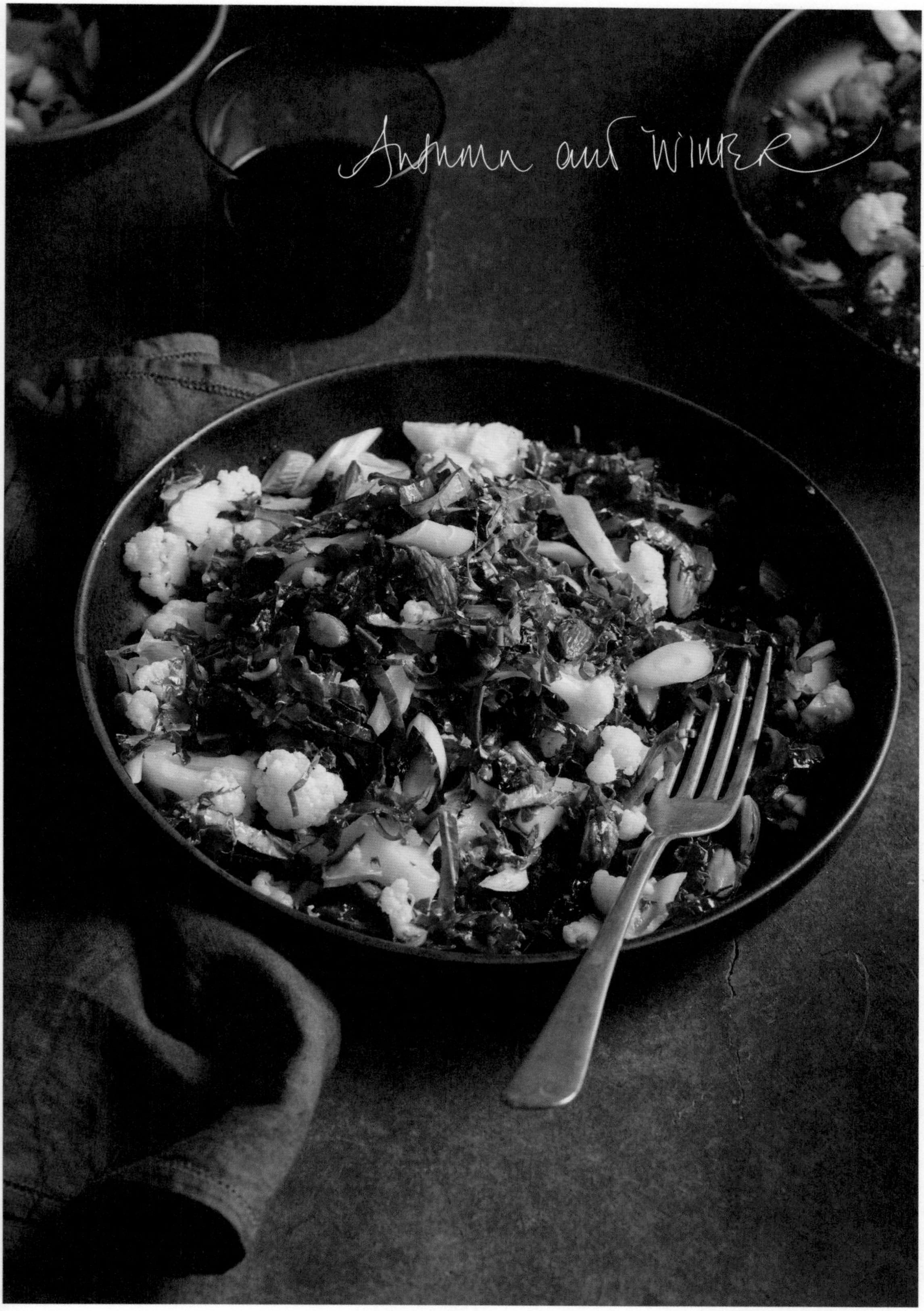
Autumn and Winter

Tomato, mozzarella & basil galette

SERVES 4–6–8 DEPENDING ON APPETITES

FOR THE SAVOURY PASTRY
200g plain flour
Pinch sea salt
100g cold butter, cubed
65–75ml chilled water
½ egg, whisked, or a little milk

FOR THE FILLING
3tbsp olive oil
500g onions, peeled and finely sliced (see page 22 for instructions)
1tsp chopped thyme
400g ripe tomatoes, cores removed and cut into large wedges
30g grated Gruyère or Cheddar cheese

TO SERVE
2 balls mozzarella, cut into small cubes
A few basil leaves, torn or cut into shreds

To make the pastry, place the flour in a large bowl with a pinch of sea salt and add the cubed butter. Using cool, clean hands, dip your fingers into the flour and rub the lumps of butter between your fingertips, and into the flour, lifting up the mixture each time as you do so, and letting it fall back into the bowl. Keep on with this action, digging deep into the bowl, making sure that all the flour gets rubbed into the butter. After a few minutes, the mixture should look like soft white breadcrumbs.

Next, using a fork, add the chilled water little by little, pulling the mixture together, creating a ball of dough. Using your hands, gently knead the dough in the bowl to make it one mass, adding a sprinkling of water if it seems too dry, or a little extra flour if it is sticky.

Gently knead the ball of dough together until it is smooth-ish – remember that over-handling the dough will result in tough, chewy pastry. Wrap the pastry in clingfilm and leave in the fridge for at least 1 hour or overnight.

Roll the pastry out into a disc approximately 3mm thick – don't worry too much about the shape at this stage – then lay on a parchment-lined baking sheet. Chill for at least 30 minutes.

Meanwhile, prepare and bake the filling ingredients. In a heavy-based shallow pan, over a medium to high heat, warm the olive oil, then fry the sliced onions until they have softened a little and turned gently golden in colour, approximately 5 minutes. Season with salt and pepper, then add the chopped thyme. Take off the heat then, using a slotted spoon, remove the onion slices to a plate.

Reheat the onion pan juices until gently sizzling, add the tomato wedges and briefly toss over the heat for a few seconds, until their edges have begun to soften.

Using a slotted spoon, remove them from the juices and allow to cool on a plate.

Heat the oven to 175°C/fan oven 155°C/mark 4.

Remove the pastry disc from the fridge and scatter the grated cheese evenly over the centre – it should cover about two thirds of the surface, leaving the rim uncovered. Next, cover the cheese evenly with the cooked onions. Scatter the tomato pieces over the top.

Carefully fold in the edges of the pastry over the filling, crimping the edges so that each section overlaps the last. This is not an exact science, and it does not have to look perfect, but the idea is to create a slightly raised wall of pastry around the filling.

Brush the crimped pastry edge with the beaten egg or milk, then bake for 35–45 minutes or until the pastry is crisp, dark golden and cooked throughout.

Remove the galette from the oven, scatter the mozzarella cubes over and sprinkle with the torn basil and a little sea salt. Serve immediately.

Rabbit with pappardelle, parsley & Parmesan

This recipe would work very well with large chicken legs instead of rabbit, if preferred. It is such a rich and comforting dish, it hardly needs anything to accompany it or to follow. But perhaps the exception could be a simple bowl of clementines in the centre of the table for dessert, for guests to peel themselves.

SERVES 4

FOR THE RABBIT
4 rabbit legs
1tsp chopped rosemary
4tbsp olive oil
1 small onion, peeled and finely diced
½ bulb fennel, finely diced
1 carrot, peeled and finely diced
2 cloves garlic, peeled and crushed
1tsp chopped thyme
200ml white wine
800ml chicken stock

TO SERVE
350g dried pappardelle or 450g fresh pappardelle
2tbsp olive oil
2tbsp roughly chopped parsley and celery leaves
40g grated Parmesan cheese

Sprinkle the rabbit legs with sea salt, freshly ground pepper and chopped rosemary. Heat 2tbsp of the olive oil in a frying pan and seal the rabbit legs until they are golden on all sides (approximately 3 minutes over a medium heat) and remove to a heavy based pan. »

Next, cook the chopped vegetables in the frying pan with the remaining 2tbsp olive oil, plus the garlic and thyme. When lightly coloured, add the wine and chicken stock. Bring to a simmer and pour the entire contents of the pan over the rabbit legs.

Simmer the meat and vegetables gently for up to 45 minutes with a tight-fitting lid, or until the meat is tender when pierced with a skewer or fork. Remove from the heat and allow to cool a little.

Remove the 4 legs to a plate and strain the juices into a large pan. Retain the vegetables and set aside. Bring the juices up to the boil and reduce by half over a high heat, to intensify the flavours.

Using a fork and spoon, remove the meat from the bones, tearing it into small pieces. Take care, as some of the bones are small. Place the meat into a bowl with the reserved vegetables and pour the warm juices over. Once cooled, this may be now left in the fridge, covered tightly, for up to 3 days.

Before serving, bring a large pan of salted water to the boil, add the pappardelle and cook until just done. Meanwhile, in a small pan heat the rabbit, vegetables and juices until piping hot, taste and adjust the seasoning if necessary.

Drain the pasta, toss with olive oil, sea salt and freshly ground pepper and tip into a warm serving dish. Pour the rabbit over the top, sprinkle with chopped parsley and celery leaves and serve immediately with grated Parmesan on the side.

Herbed & spiced meatballs

While these may be accompanied by crisp roasted potatoes, a green vegetable and a dollop of mustard, they can also be served in a tomato soup (see photo and page 188) or with 'baked beans' (see page 220), which would turn the dish into a nourishing, warming and most satisfying main meal. Simply add to the soup with the kale or place them into a warm serving bowl and ladle the beans over, offering everyone a large spoon and fork.

SERVES 2 AS A MAIN MEAL
OR 4 IN THE SOUP
300g lean mince, either lamb,
  pork or beef
½tsp ground cumin
1 clove garlic, peeled and crushed
1 small chilli, finely chopped

½tsp ground coriander
½tsp ground fennel seeds
1tbsp chopped coriander, mint
  or parsley leaves
½tsp sea salt
Vegetable or olive oil, for frying

Place the mince in a bowl with the remaining ingredients (except the oil) and mix well – this is best done using your hands, but wash them thoroughly before and afterwards. Alternatively, a good strong wooden spoon will do the trick.

Shape the meat into 8–12 balls and leave in the fridge, for up to 3 days, tightly covered with clingfilm. (Warning – the garlic fumes will easily escape into your fridge unless the meatballs are well covered.)

Heat a splash of oil over a high heat in a heavy-based frying pan and cook the meatballs by turning them over, making sure all surfaces are sealed and that they turn a nice dark brown. Turn the heat down a little to cook them through on the insides. This should take 3–4 minutes total.

These would also work well with warm herbed lentils and a salad of crisp leaves, toasted nuts and raisins, tossed with lemon, oil, salt and pepper.

Soup of tomato, curly kale & chickpeas

SERVES 4–5

FOR THE CHICKPEAS
100g dried chickpeas (or 1 x 400g can chickpeas)
½ onion, peeled
1 stick celery
1 carrot, peeled and cut in half lengthwise
2 bay leaves or 1 sprig rosemary
½tsp bicarbonate of soda
1tsp sea salt

FOR THE SOUP
6 ripe medium round or plum tomatoes (or 1 x 400g can
  peeled tomatoes)
1 onion, peeled and halved
2 sticks celery
1 bulb fennel
150g curly kale or 1 small green cabbage
3tbsp olive oil, plus a little for finishing
1 clove garlic, peeled and crushed
1 small chilli, sliced fine or chopped
1 litre vegetable, chickpea or chicken stock
1tsp sea salt
Roughly chopped celery, parsley or coriander leaves, to serve
Crusty bread, to serve

Soak the dried chickpeas overnight in plenty of cold water. The following day, place the chickpeas and the water in a pan and bring to the boil. Drain, rinse and place into a clean pan with enough fresh water to cover them well. Add the vegetables, herbs and bicarbonate of soda. Bring to the boil, then simmer for up to 1 hour or until the chickpeas are well cooked, topping up the water if needed.

Remove the chickpeas from the heat and add the sea salt, then allow to cool in their liquid. Drain them and retain the liquid for future use, for example for use in a vegetable stock. Alternatively, drain and rinse the canned chickpeas before using.

Meanwhile, prepare the remaining ingredients for the soup:

If using fresh tomatoes, peel the skins away (see page 24) and discard. Cut the tomatoes into medium-sized chunks and leave on one side, including all the juices.

Slice the onion, celery and fennel as fine as possible (see page 23). Shred the kale or cabbage medium-fine.

In a heavy-based pan, heat the 3tbsp olive oil with the garlic and chili, stirring over a medium heat for 1–2 minutes until gently sizzling – do not allow the garlic to colour.

Add the sliced onion, celery and fennel and continue to stir as they soften and turn golden at the edges, approximately 4–5 minutes. Add the drained chickpeas, the stock and salt, then add the tomatoes (fresh or canned), and bring gently to the boil.

Simmer for up to 30 minutes, or until the flavour is to your liking.

Add the shredded kale or cabbage and cook gently until wilted (about 2–3 minutes) and then, just before removing from the heat, add the leaves of celery, parsley or coriander and taste for seasoning.

Serve with slices of warm, crusty bread that have been drizzled with olive oil and sprinkled with sea salt.

Alternatively, if you prefer to keep the soup for a day or two, remove from the heat, allow to cool completely, then cover it and store in the fridge for up to 3 days.

Photo shows the addition of Herbed & spiced meatballs (page 185). For this, simply add the hot meatballs to the pan with the shredded kale or cabbage and continue as above.

Dinner alone

Unusually for a restaurateur (or maybe precisely
because of it!) I rather relish the thought
of peace and quiet from time to time.
Turn on a beautiful piece of music, light a candle,
unfold the napkin and breathe in deeply...

Spring and Summer

Whipped cream cheese with baked toasts
Polentina soup with Parmesan
Pasta with summer vegetables, basil and pine nuts

Autumn and Winter

Chicken liver and honey pâté
Chopped salad
Apple Brown Betty

Whipped cream cheese

This recipe makes enough for 4 greedy people, or a few more if offered with other 'nibbles', but it is also a lovely 'stop-gap' if one is eating alone, served with the toasts and alongside a soup or salad.

250g cream cheese, goat's curd or ricotta
80g sour cream
1 clove garlic, peeled and crushed
½tsp finely chopped thyme leaves

1tbsp finely chopped parsley leaves
1tbsp finely chopped chives or spring onions
A little good olive oil

Using a wooden spoon in a medium bowl, mix the cream cheese, goat's curd or ricotta with the sour cream until smooth. Stir in the garlic, a little sea salt and freshly ground pepper and the chopped thyme and parsley. Taste and scoop into a serving bowl.

Cover tightly and leave in the fridge for up to 24 hours before scattering the top with the chives or spring onions and a drizzle of olive oil. Serve.

Baked toasts for scooping or spreading

¼ baguette or other small loaf
Olive oil

Heat the oven to 170°C/fan oven 150°C/mark 3. Cut the baguette across into thin slices, lay overlapping on a baking sheet and drizzle with olive oil. If using a large loaf, slice as finely as possible and cut each slice into 2 or 4, depending on the size.

Sprinkle with sea salt and freshly ground pepper and bake for about 5–7 minutes, turning over halfway through cooking if necessary, or until crisp and golden on both sides.

Serve with the whipped cream cheese or with chicken liver pâté (see page 200), soups or stews.

Spring and Summer

Polentina soup with Parmesan

This is possibly my favourite soup. It has the most wonderful comforting and nourishing effect and is perfect for an early spring evening. A lovely addition to this could be sliced field mushrooms, quickly sautéed in a pan until soft and juicy, with a little olive oil, parsley and crushed garlic. Scatter them into the bowl over the top of the soup.

SERVES 1
300ml vegetable, chicken or light meat stock
40g polenta
2tbsp olive oil, plus extra for drizzling
2tsp butter
25g grated Parmesan cheese
A few sprigs watercress, stalks removed, washed and spun dry
Spoonful double cream or crème fraîche (optional), to serve
Crusty bread, soda bread (see page 77) or granary bread (see page 39),
   to serve

Bring the stock to the boil in a heavy-based pan and very slowly pour in the polenta, whisking over a medium heat.

Once the polenta has all been absorbed, gently simmer for 10–15 minutes or until the soup has thickened and the polenta has softened and no longer tastes gritty.

Remove the soup from the heat, season with sea salt and freshly ground pepper, and stir in the olive oil, butter and, finally, half the grated Parmesan. Taste for seasoning and leave covered on one side.

In a bowl, toss the watercress with a drizzle of olive oil, salt and pepper.

Ladle the soup into a warm bowl and scatter with watercress and the remaining Parmesan. Pour over a little double cream or crème fraîche, if using, and serve with warm bread.

Pasta with summer vegetables, basil & pine nuts

In the summer you have such a wide variety of vegetables and salad leaves to choose from, all of which marry perfectly with the pasta of your choice. Pull it all together with this most summery of sauces, a classic basil pesto. The pesto is best used on the day it is made, but if you wish to save it for another day, pour into a jam jar with a lid and keep in the fridge for up to 2 weeks. This recipe will make much more than you will need for one serving of pasta, but you will be able to enjoy the leftovers for a few days to come.

SERVES 1 WITH LOTS OF LEFTOVERS

FOR THE PESTO
60g pine nuts
250ml olive oil
2 cloves garlic, peeled and crushed to a cream
Small bunch basil leaves, approximately 40g
Small bunch parsley leaves, approximately 30g
75g grated Parmesan cheese

FOR THE PASTA
A few handfuls any of the following: freshly podded peas, asparagus
  or broccoli spears (sliced on the angle) and trimmed green beans
85g dried pasta
2tbsp olive oil
1tbsp grated Parmesan cheese, to serve
A few basil or parsley leaves, to serve

First, make the pesto. The best way is to make it all by hand as described below – chopping everything separately, then mixing it all with the olive oil to the consistency you want, and to your taste. »

Finely chop the pine nuts and place them in a pan with 125ml of the olive oil. Cook over a low heat, stirring a little, for 1 minute, until they have turned golden and smell wonderful. Take care, as they will burn easily.

Remove from the heat, add the garlic, season with sea salt and freshly ground pepper and leave to cool. Chop the basil and parsley together medium fine and place in a bowl. Add the cooled pine nuts and the cooking oil, the remaining 125ml olive oil, to taste, and the Parmesan and stir gently together. Taste and leave on one side. See photo opposite.

Prepare the vegetables and cook the pasta of your choice according to the packet instructions in boiling salted water. Test the pasta for doneness and when you feel it is almost ready (1–2 minutes before), add the raw vegetables and give it all a good stir. Bring back to the boil and continue to cook until the pasta and vegetables are cooked.

Keeping a little of the cooking water, drain the pasta and vegetables through a colander or sieve and return them to the pan over a medium heat with the reserved water.

Add the olive oil and a little sea salt and pepper, stir well, pour into a warm serving bowl and drizzle with some of the pesto. Sprinkle the pasta with the grated Parmesan, scatter with the leaves of parsley or basil and serve immediately.

Any leftovers may be kept in the fridge and served cold for lunch the following day.

Chicken liver & honey pâté

While this recipe makes enough for many more than one, it is lovely to have a pot of this sitting in the fridge for a day or two, to dip into either as a snack in between meals or as a light main course, if one is eating alone.

500g chicken livers
50g butter
1 clove garlic, peeled and crushed
1 shallot or small onion, peeled
  and very finely sliced

2 bay leaves
1tsp honey
Celery sticks, radishes, gherkins
  and/or spring onions, to serve

Trim away the sinew and/or discoloured parts from the livers, then rinse in cold water and drain well.

In a pan, gently warm the butter, garlic and shallot (or onion) together over a medium heat with some sea salt and freshly ground pepper and the bay leaves, until soft.

Add the livers and stir until the outsides are sealed (approximately 2–3 minutes). Do not cook the livers completely through as you want to end up with a lovely soft pâté that is slightly pink. Remove the bay leaves.

Pour the contents of the pan into a liquidiser, add the honey and purée until very smooth. Taste and adjust the seasoning and place everything into a small serving pot. Press the pâté down gently so that it is compact within the pot, allow to cool and cover tightly with a lid or clingfilm. The butter will usually separate a little from the livers and create a natural seal on top of the pâté. This can either be removed when you serve it or simply scooped with the livers straight onto toasts or bread.

Serve with celery sticks, radishes, gherkins or spring onions, or a mixture of all, plus toasted bread or baked toasts (see page 192).

Autumn and Winter

Chopped salad

Those TV chefs make it all look so easy, but with a bit of practice, you too could chop like a pro. Chopping most ingredients into a small neat dice is really not that difficult. This salad takes a bit of time to prepare but it is very satisfying to serve and relatively quick to eat. Always have a little extra dressing or mayonnaise to serve on the side. Choose as few or as many of the following ingredients as you would like to include, in the quantities you feel like.

Roasted chicken breast (see page 172)
Swiss cheese
Cooked ham or crisp streaky bacon
Large beefsteak or cherry tomatoes
Celery
Cucumber
Courgette
Red, green or yellow pepper
Crisp lettuce, such as cos or little gem
Carrot, peeled and coarsely grated
Avocado

FOR THE DRESSING
6tbsp good-quality olive oil or 2tbsp mayonnaise (see page 79)
1tbsp lemon juice

First, make the dressing. Either mix the olive oil with 1tbsp lemon juice and some sea salt and freshly ground pepper until smooth, or mix 2tbsp homemade mayonnaise with 1tbsp lemon juice, a splash of cold water and some seasoning to make it a pouring consistency.

Using a large, sharp, heavy knife and a clean, level chopping board (see page 22), slice the chicken evenly, then layer the slices on top of one another. Slice again lengthwise, creating batons. Then gather the batons » together in a straight line and slice across neatly, creating small squares. Do the same with the cheese and the ham or bacon.

Peel away the skin of the tomato (see page 24) and discard. Cut into quarters, scoop out the seeds and place the petals of tomato on the chopping board. One by one, cut each into 4 or 5 strips, line up together and cut across, making small, neat squares. (Retain the seeds and skin for another use, such as soup or stock).

Cut the celery, cucumber and courgette into batons also, then cut across into neat dice.

The easiest way to dice a pepper is to first cut off the sides that are straight, then cut those into batons, then across. The trimmings of the pepper may then also be cut into dice in the same way.

Remove the base of the lettuce, releasing the leaves, then wash and shred them finely with a sharp knife. Peel and grate the carrot.

The avocado needs to be medium-ripe but still firm enough to cut into dice, and should be cut last, as it is the most delicate ingredient and will discolour easily.

Place all the ingredients onto a plate, lined up attractively so that the colours and shapes complement each other, then drizzle over half the dressing.

Alternatively, mix all the ingredients together in a bowl (except the avocado) and toss gently with half the dressing. Pile attractively onto the serving plate, then scatter the avocado over.

Serve the remaining dressing and/or mayonnaise on the side.

Apple Brown Betty

I first published this recipe in 1999, and it remains one of my favourite winter desserts. It is warming, comforting, sweet and slightly sharp, crunchy and soft, all at the same time.

MAKES ENOUGH FOR 4–6
FOR THE TOPPING
100g fresh breadcrumbs (see below
  for method)
35g butter
35g demerara sugar
1½tsp ground cinnamon
½tsp mixed spice

FOR THE APPLE PURÉE
1kg Bramley apples, peeled, cored
  and roughly chopped
20g butter
100g sugar
Whipped cream or vanilla
  ice cream, to serve

First, make the breadcrumbs. Trim away most of the crust and cut the bread into cubes. Liquidise in small batches until crumbed. Ideally you want small to medium clumps – not at all fine in texture. In the absence of a liquidiser, chop the cubes by hand until small.

To make the topping, heat the butter in a wide-based pan and fry the crumbs, stirring constantly until golden and crunchy (taking great care, as they will burn easily). Just as they begin to turn a pleasing mid-dark golden colour, remove from the heat and add the sugar and spices. Stir well together and leave in a warm place.

Place the apples in a small saucepan with enough water to cover the base of the pan. Add the butter and sugar and cover with a lid. Cook over a medium heat, shaking the pan occasionally so that the apples cook evenly. I prefer a few lumps to remain in the purée, but completely smooth is also fine if you prefer. This will take about 10–15 minutes cooking time.

Spoon the warm apple purée into warm serving bowls and scatter with the spiced crumbs. Serve as soon as possible with whipped cream or vanilla ice cream.

Dinner with everyone

As I write this mid-pandemic, there is a tear in my eye.
The memories of friends and families gathered around a table
to break bread, and much more, are distant, but those happy times will
surely return. Invitations will be flung far and wide, and gathering
will become part of our lives again.

Spring and Summer

Pea, mint and potato frittata with a salad of herbs
Spiced lamb koftas with yogurt, mint and cucumber
Warm chickpeas with spinach
Strawberry ripple ice cream

Autumn and Winter

Pain perdu with pecans
Baked beans with vegetables and herbs
Braised duck legs in orange and rosemary with celeriac mash
Spiced chard leaves

Pea, mint & potato frittata with a salad of herbs

This is a perfect dish for using leftover potatoes, peas, courgettes or almost any other vegetables. Left cold, it makes a very lovely addition to a picnic or, wrapped in greaseproof paper, it could make a welcome mid-morning snack at a lonely desk or a snack on the run the next day.

SERVES 4, NORMALLY WITH A LITTLE LEFT OVER
4tbsp olive oil
350g cooked potatoes, cut into walnut-sized chunks
1 onion, peeled and finely sliced
6 free-range or organic eggs
1tbsp chopped mint, chives or parsley
A few cooked vegetables, such as sliced asparagus or courgette, peas or broccoli cut into florets

TO SERVE
40g grated Parmesan cheese
A few small salad leaves or herbs, such as parsley, chopped chives or celery leaves
Sour cream

Heat the olive oil in a heavy-based non-stick ovenproof frying pan until smoking hot, add the potato and onion and fry until almost golden, tossing occasionally.

Whisk the eggs with the herbs and some sea salt and freshly ground pepper until very frothy and pour over the potatoes. Shake the pan to distribute the potatoes evenly.

Turn the heat down and cook for 4–6 minutes or until the egg is golden on the underside. (Gently lift an edge up with a wooden spoon to check »

Spring and Summer

the doneness after a few minutes). Meanwhile, turn the overhead grill on.

Sprinkle the cooked vegetables over the frittata, and gently press them into the surface using a spoon.

Place under the grill and cook for a further 2–3 minutes or until the egg is cooked through. Check by pressing the centre with a spoon – if the egg is still liquid, it will need a few more minutes. Remove from the heat and allow to settle a little as it cools.

Now, for the tricky bit. If the frittata has not stuck to the base, slide it out of the pan carefully on to a warm serving platter. If it does not readily free itself, place the platter inverted over the pan. Holding the pan handle carefully with an oven cloth in one hand and the plate firmly with the other, turn the two over together. This will result in the frittata being placed upside-down on the platter.

If the frittata has stuck to the inside of the pan, very gently nudge the underneath of the frittata away from the pan base with a thin, flexible implement, such as a palette knife or fish slice, without scratching the pan's surface.

Sprinkle the frittata with grated Parmesan, salad leaves or herb leaves and serve sliced into wedges, warm or cool, with a scoop of sour cream.

Spiced lamb koftas with yogurt, mint & cucumber

This recipe is lovely used as a picnic idea too. Simply cool the skewered lamb as quickly as possible and leave well covered in the fridge for up to 3 days. Take to the park with the cucumber dressing in a little pot and some flatbreads or ciabatta.

SERVES 6

FOR THE KOFTAS
1tsp cumin seeds (or ½tsp ground)
1tsp coriander seeds (or ½tsp ground)
1tsp fennel seeds (or ½tsp ground)
750g lean lamb mince (ideally from the leg)
2 cloves garlic, peeled and crushed
1 small red or green chilli, finely chopped
1 small orange, grated zest
1tbsp chopped parsley
1tsp chopped coriander, marjoram or mint
1tsp sea salt

FOR THE CUCUMBER DRESSING
½ cucumber
250g plain yogurt
½ lemon, juice
1tsp finely chopped mint

TO SERVE
Salad leaves tossed with olive oil, salt, pepper and a squeeze of lemon
Flatbreads or ciabatta
Lemon wedges
Warm chickpeas with spinach (see page 214)

Soak 12 thick wooden skewers in water while you make the koftas. (This will prevent the wood from burning in the oven.)

Place the spices (whole or ground) in a small pan and warm over a medium heat for a few seconds, until they smell fragrant. If using whole spices, grind them until fine using an electric grinder or a pestle and mortar. Leave to cool.

Mix the lamb mince with the cooled ground spices, garlic, chilli, orange zest, chopped herbs and salt in a large bowl – I prefer to do this by hand, but remember to wash your hands thoroughly before and afterwards.

Divide into 12 and mould into sausage shapes. Press one end of a skewer along the length of each sausage and shape the meat around the skewer neatly and tightly. If covered tightly on a plate with clingfilm, the koftas will keep for up to 2 days in the fridge before cooking.

If you have a grill within the oven, heat it to its highest setting. Line a baking sheet with aluminium foil, then line up the koftas on the baking sheet, covering the exposed end of each skewer with a small piece of foil. Grill until the koftas are dark golden in colour (about 3–4 minutes), then turn them over and grill again in the same way until they are almost cooked through (approximately a further 2–3 minutes). Turn the grill off and leave them in the oven with the door closed to finish cooking and to keep warm.

If you are using an oven without a grill, heat it to 200°C/fan oven 180°C/mark 6 and roast on the lined baking sheet for 10–12 minutes, turning halfway through the cooking.

If you have a barbecue, even better – grill the koftas on one side over a high heat, turn them over and then move them to a cooler spot to cook them through. This should take no more than 5–6 minutes.

Meanwhile, make the cucumber dressing. Grate the cucumber on the largest side of a cheese grater and place in a medium bowl with the yogurt, lemon juice and a little sea salt and freshly ground pepper. Mix together well, then add the finely chopped mint.

Serve the hot lamb skewers with the cucumber dressing, flatbreads, lemon wedges and a salad or with the following recipe for chickpeas and spinach.

Warm chickpeas with spinach

SERVES 4–6

300g dried chickpeas (or 2 x 400g
  cans chickpeas)
1tsp bicarbonate of soda
1 small onion, peeled and cut into 4
1 small carrot, peeled and cut in
  half lengthwise
1 stick celery, cut into large chunks
A few bay leaves

4tbsp olive oil
1 clove garlic, peeled and crushed
A few handfuls spinach leaves,
  stalks removed, washed well
  and drained (though not dry)
1 red chilli, finely chopped
  (optional)
1 lemon, juice

If using dried chickpeas, soak them overnight, well covered with cold
water, in a cool place. The following day, tip them with the water into a
large pan and bring to the boil rapidly. Drain and rinse with cold water,
then place them in a clean pan and cover with fresh cold water to at
least twice their depth. Add the bicarbonate of soda, vegetables and bay
leaves. Do not add salt as it will toughen the outer skin of the chickpeas.

Bring to the boil, then turn down the heat and simmer, covered, for
60–90 minutes or until a chickpea is easily squashed between your
fingers. They should not be at all undercooked. Season with salt only
once they are fully cooked. Allow to cool in the broth, then drain
(reserving the liquid) and remove the vegetables and bay leaves.

Keep the liquid for another use, for example in vegetable soups, stews,
risotto or for thinning a sauce. Once chilled, it will keep in the fridge for
up to 5 days. If using canned chickpeas, simply drain them and continue
with the method from this point.

To serve, heat the olive oil and garlic in a frying pan until gently sizzling
and fragrant. Add the chickpeas and toss over a high heat for a few
minutes until thoroughly hot. Add the spinach leaves and stir together
over the heat as the leaves wilt. Season with sea salt and freshly ground
pepper (or finely chopped red chilli, if using). Add the lemon juice at the
last second and pour the contents of the pan into a warm serving dish.
Serve as soon as possible.

Strawberry ripple ice cream

This is a fail safe, if slightly cheating, method for making a delicious ice cream with hardly any effort at all. You just need a little time and a good freezer.

SERVES 4
1 x 500g tub good-quality vanilla ice cream
400g ripe strawberries
1tsp lemon juice
2tsp caster sugar
Meringues (see page 130) or shortbread (see page 259), to serve

Firstly, make sure that the freezer is empty enough to comfortably hold a shallow container for the mixed ice cream, with lots of space around it.

Remove the vanilla ice cream from the freezer and allow it to come to room temperature around the outside. This will take approximately 5–10 minutes, depending on the weather.

Meanwhile, remove the green leaves from the strawberries. Set aside 4 of the best ones, tipping the rest into a large bowl with the lemon juice and sugar. Squash together with a fork until they resemble a lumpy mess.

Add the ice cream to the bowl and continue to mix with the fork, breaking up the ice cream a little. It should become creamy with lumps of strawberry throughout but not liquid. Speed is of the essence here – do not allow the ice cream to become too soft. As quickly as possible, pour the mixture into the shallow container and cover tightly with clingfilm. Freeze until almost solid again, allowing at least 2–3 hours for most domestic freezers.

Scoop or slice the ice cream and serve with meringues, shortbread or just by itself with the reserved strawberries, cut in half, as decoration.

Pain perdu with pecans

The name of this dish means 'lost bread' in French. It is a good way to 'rescue' day-old bread that might otherwise go to waste, using eggs, cream, milk, spices and sugar. Sliced fruit, such as strawberries or bananas, make a good addition or could replace the bacon.

SERVES 4

100g butter, softened
½ baguette or small white loaf
3 large free-range or organic eggs
2tbsp double cream
200ml milk
2tbsp soft brown sugar

½tsp cinnamon
Pinch salt
1tbsp chopped pecans
8 rashers smoked streaky bacon
  (optional)
Maple syrup or honey, to serve

Heat the oven to 190 °C/fan oven 170°C/mark 5. Using your clean fingers, smear the inside of a shallow ovenproof dish with the soft butter.

Slice the bread thickly and cut each slice into half or quarters, depending on the size of the loaf.

Whisk the eggs in a bowl with the cream, milk, half the sugar, cinnamon and salt until fluffy. Dip the bread slices into the bowl, one by one, allowing them to soak for a few seconds each time and gently turning over each slice until completely covered.

Lay the bread into the buttered dish, with the slices slightly overlapping one another neatly, crusts uppermost. Pour any remaining liquid over the slices, sprinkle with the remaining sugar and then with the pecans.

Cover the dish with aluminium foil and bake for 10–15 minutes, then remove the foil and continue to bake for 8–10 minutes or until the edges are golden and the sugar is crunchy, taking care that the nuts don't burn.

Meanwhile, place the bacon rashers (if using) in a shallow pan and cook over a medium to high heat, on both sides until crisp. Remove the dish from the oven and serve the pain perdu scooped onto warm plates, with the bacon on the top and the maple syrup or honey drizzled over.

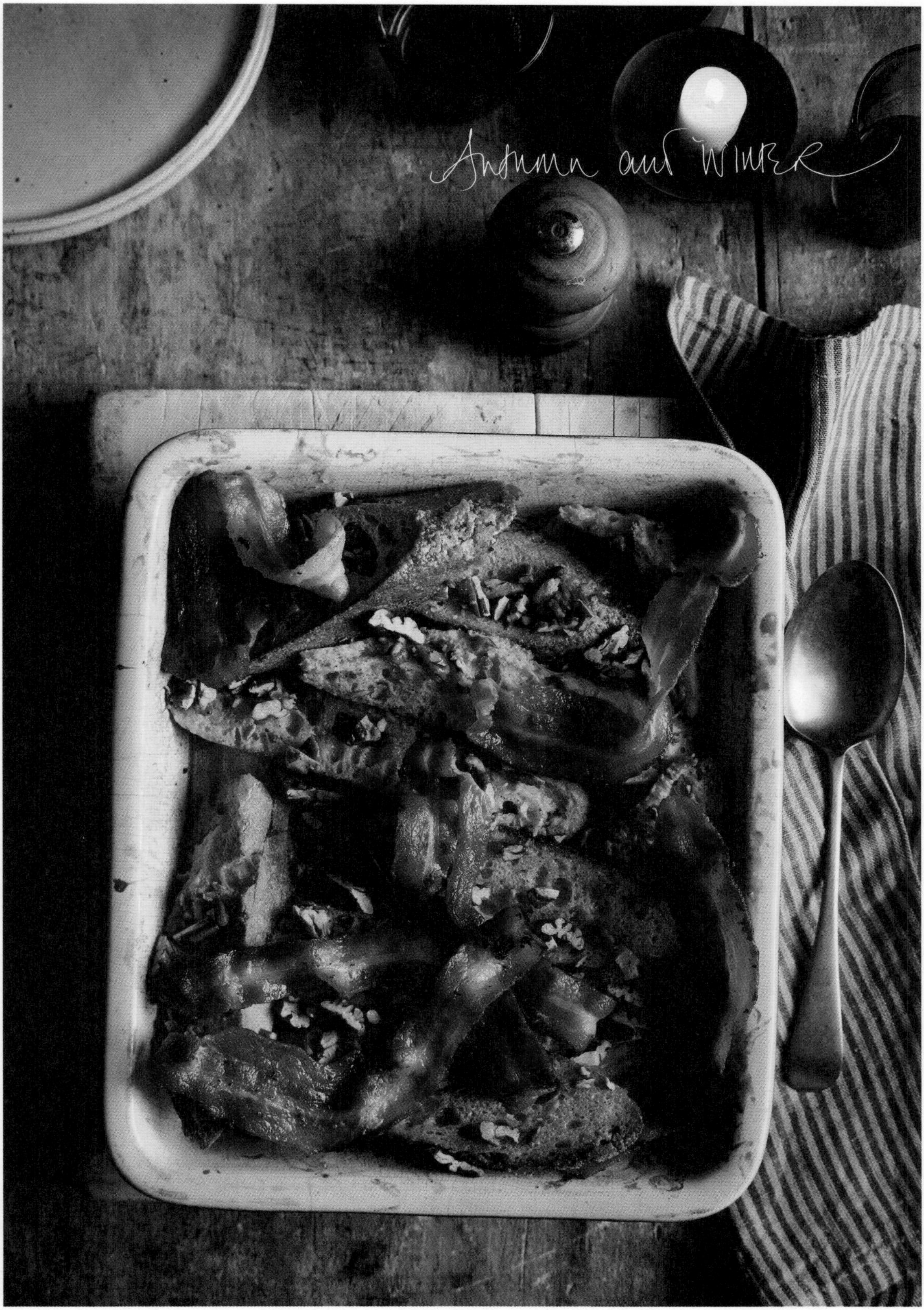
Autumn and Winter

'Baked beans' with vegetables & herbs

Of course you can cheat if you want. Buy canned haricot beans, either green or white, or canned chickpeas – any of these will halve if not quarter your preparation time (preferably do not choose red kidney beans for this). Or you could make your own baked beans properly as follows. This makes a hearty and pleasing vegetarian dish but it could also be served with the herbed and spiced meatballs (see page 185) or the lamb koftas, once removed from their skewers (see page 211).

SERVES 4
300g dried white cannellini beans or similar beans
½tsp bicarbonate of soda
½ onion, peeled and cut in 2, plus 1 small onion, peeled and finely diced
1 carrot, peeled and cut in 2 lengthwise
1 stick celery, cut into 3 or 4 pieces
1 sprig bay, rosemary or thyme
1 clove garlic, peeled and crushed
Olive oil, for frying
1tsp mixed chopped herbs, such as rosemary, thyme or sage
4 large ripe tomatoes, peeled (see page 24) and roughly chopped
  or 1 x 400g tin chopped tomatoes

Soak the dried beans in a bowl in a cool place overnight, well covered with cold water. Tip the beans and water into a large saucepan and bring to the boil rapidly. Drain the beans, rinse with cold water, then place them in a clean saucepan and cover with fresh cold water to at least twice their depth.

Add the bicarbonate of soda, ½ onion, carrot and celery and the sprig of bay, rosemary or thyme – save the diced onion for later. Do not add salt at this stage, as it will toughen the outer skin of the beans. Bring to the boil, then turn down the heat. Cover, then simmer for 60–90 minutes (depending on the bean). When they are cooked, you will be able to easily squash one between your fingers. They should not be at all undercooked – a tiny bit overcooked is better than under.

Pick out the herb sprig and discard. Remove the vegetables with a fork or tongs to a chopping board. Cut them into small bite-sized pieces and add them back to the beans. Season the beans with salt, to taste, and leave to cool in the liquid.

Drain the beans and vegetables through a sieve, retaining the juices, which may be used as vegetable stock for soups, stews or other similar dishes.

Meanwhile, in a large heavy-based saucepan, cook the garlic and diced onion in a drizzle of olive oil for 2–3 minutes or until pale golden. Add the mixed chopped herbs and the chopped tomatoes and simmer for a few minutes, until the aroma is pleasing.

Next add the drained beans and vegetables, plus enough of the liquid to make a soupy mixture. Bring to the boil and simmer for 10–15 minutes. Taste for seasoning and pour into a warm serving dish.

Once cold, the beans may be left in the fridge, well covered, for up to 5 days.

Braised duck legs in orange & rosemary with celeriac mash

SERVES 4

FOR THE BRAISED DUCK LEGS
4 large duck legs
2 teaspoons finely chopped rosemary
2 cloves garlic, peeled and crushed with salt
2tbsp vegetable oil
1 onion, peeled and chopped
1 large carrot, peeled and sliced
1 stick celery, sliced
2 outer leaves fennel, sliced
2 bay leaves
1 large orange, peel and juice
700ml chicken, duck or meat stock
1 large glass full-bodied red wine (optional)
A few chopped celery or parsley leaves, to serve

FOR THE CELERIAC MASH
2 large potatoes, peeled, then cut into walnut-sized pieces
½ large celeriac, peeled, then cut into walnut-sized pieces
50ml milk
25g butter
Finely sliced spring onion or finely chopped chives

Trim away the excess fat and skin around the edges of the duck legs and
season well with sea salt, freshly ground pepper and half the rosemary
and garlic. Using your hands, massage the seasoning into the meat and
fatty side of the legs. Leave, covered, on one side at room temperature for
at least 2 hours or preferably overnight. Wash and dry your hands well.

Heat the oven to 170 °C/fan oven 150 °C/mark 4. When the oven is hot,
place the duck legs in a shallow, heavy-based ovenproof saucepan or »

casserole with a splash of vegetable oil, skin-side down, and cook on the hob over a medium to high heat until the fat starts to run and the skin turns golden brown. Using tongs, turn the legs over and seal the other side for 12 minutes. Remove from the pan.

Next, add the vegetables to the pan and cook over a medium to high heat until they start to soften and turn pale golden at the edges. Add the bay leaves, orange peel and the remaining rosemary and garlic. Pour in the stock, wine (if using) and orange juice and bring to a gentle simmer.

Place the duck legs on top of the vegetables, skin side up, cover the pan with a lid or aluminium foil and then place in the oven and cook for 20–25 minutes. Carefully take the pan out of the oven – the meat will have taken on some colour and the juices will be bubbling around the edges. If the level of liquid is above that of the duck, pour a little away and leave on one side until later.

Place the pan back in the oven, uncovered, and braise for 50–60 minutes further, or until the skin is beautifully crisp and a deep golden colour. A small, sharp knife should pierce the meat easily, with no resistance when pulling the knife away.

Meanwhile, bring a saucepan of salted water to a boil, add the potatoes and celeriac and cook until tender. Drain and return to the pan. Add the milk and butter, season with salt and pepper and then mash until smooth. Leave in a warm place while you finish the duck.

Remove the duck legs to a warm serving dish. Strain the juices into a small pan and, after a few minutes of cooling, skim away the fat that has risen to the surface. (The best looking pieces of vegetables remaining could now be arranged around the duck.) Cover the dish tightly and keep warm.

Bring the juices rapidly to the boil (including those reserved earlier, if any) and reduce by a third or until it is to your taste, adjusting the seasoning if necessary.

Taste the celeriac mash, stir in the chopped chives or spring onion and then scoop into a warm dish.

Uncover the serving dish, scatter the duck generously with chopped celery or parsley leaves and serve the sauce on the side with the celeriac mash.

Spiced chard leaves

Use either white and green chard or the red, yellow, pink and pale green varieties sold together as rainbow chard – often in mixed bunches in markets.

SERVES 4
1 large bunch chard
4tbsp olive oil
1 small chilli, finely chopped
2 cloves garlic, peeled and crushed

Trim away the base of the chard stalks and discard. Wash the leaves well, then cut the stalks from the leaves in a V shape. Cut the stalks across in 1cm slices and gently tear the leaf parts into 2, 3 or 4 pieces, depending on the size.

Bring a saucepan of salted water to a boil and blanch the stalks for 1–2 minutes or until they have lost their crispness, then drain.

In a large, heavy-based saucepan, heat the olive oil, chilli and garlic until sizzling and fragrant. Add the blanched chard stalks and toss over a high heat for a few minutes or until they have coloured a little. Add the leaves, a little salt and a splash of water and toss gently together.

Cover the pan with a lid and cook for 3–4 minutes or until the chard leaves have wilted slightly. Serve as soon as possible, although this dish is equally delicious served at room temperature or even cold as a salad.

Dinner to impress

To many, the thought of having to prepare a meal 'to impress'
a potential love, a new boss or even a set of possible in-laws
is daunting. There are also the various dinner party hosts who
desperately try to out-do one another with successive acts of bravado!
However, the trick here is to not try too hard.
Relax, breathe deeply, plan ahead, make lists – and enjoy it!

Spring and Summer

Chilled carrot soup with yogurt, coriander and cumin wafer toasts
Herb-filled chicken breasts with wild rice salad and citrus dressing
Baked fillet of plaice with chervil and spring onion
Pavlova meringue with strawberries and spring rhubarb

Autumn and Winter

Cheddar, sweetcorn and basil soufflé
Brussels sprouts with pecans, lemon zest and butter
Comice pear, Comté, walnut and lemon salad
Braised pheasant with soft Parmesan polenta, chestnuts & raisins

Chilled carrot soup with yogurt, coriander & cumin wafer toasts

A soup is one of the easiest first courses to prepare and serve, as most preparation can be done well in advance, which allows the cook time to concentrate on the details of the rest of the menu.

This recipe could form the base of many different flavours – depending on the time of the year and which vegetables are available to you. For example, celeriac or parsnip in the winter or perhaps tomatoes, courgette, red or yellow peppers in the summer could replace the carrot.

It is worth noting here that the carrot provides an element of 'starch' to the soup, which helps in 'thickening' the texture as it is puréed. For this reason, you may need to add a little potato to the onion and celery base if using vegetables with a high water content, such as courgettes or peppers.

Our Production Kitchen, which is based just a stone's throw away from the Restaurant, creates a daily-rotating selection of soups for sale in our shops; fennel with lemon, minestrone, beetroot with apple or spinach, for example. The recipes for these were originally created in the Restaurant, and have proved to be amongst the most popular items in our range of takeaway dishes chosen by our customers. So if time is short for you, and you are close by – you could always 'cheat' by choosing one of ours, ready made for you! »

Spring and Summer

SERVES 4–6

5 tbsp olive oil, plus extra for
  the toasts
2 cloves garlic, peeled and crushed
1 small chilli, halved lengthwise
1 onion, peeled and sliced
2 sticks celery, chopped
1 rounded tsp ground cumin, plus
  extra for the toasts

1 tsp ground coriander
800g carrots, peeled and sliced
  into medium-sized chunks
A few coriander stalks
  (reserve leaves for garnish)
¼ baguette (preferably a day old)
Plain yogurt, to serve

In a large pan, heat the olive oil with the garlic, chilli, onion, celery and spices. Cook over a medium heat until the aroma of the spices is fragrant and the vegetables have started to soften (approximately 3–5 minutes).

Season with salt and add the carrots, coriander stalks and water to barely cover, and bring to the boil. Cover with a lid and simmer for 20–25 minutes or until the vegetables are all very soft.

Place the vegetables (without the liquid) in a liquidiser and purée until smooth, adding the liquid little by little until the correct consistency is reached. Use a ladle to push the soup through a medium-gauge sieve into a large bowl, and discard the debris.

Alternatively, if a liquidiser or food processor is not available, you may like to serve this as a chunky soup. Remove the herb stalks, then simply crush the vegetables in the pan using a potato masher.

Taste for seasoning and consistency and leave to cool to room temperature. You can now store the soup, covered, in the fridge for up to 5 days (as with most soups, the flavour is at its best on day one.)

When you are ready to serve, heat the oven to 160°C/fan oven 140 °C/mark 3. Slice the day-old baguette finely (about 3–4 slices per person) and lay them overlapping on a baking tray. Drizzle with olive oil and sprinkle with a little cumin, salt and freshly ground pepper. Bake for 5–7 minutes or until golden, then turn over and bake for 2–3 minutes.

To serve, check the consistency of the soup is to your liking, then pour into bowls, top with a scoop of yogurt, scatter with coriander leaves and serve with the wafer toasts. If you prefer to serve the soup hot, simply bring it carefully to the boil, check the consistency and serve as above.

Herb-filled chicken breasts with wild rice salad & citrus dressing

Choose one or two herbs that you like the look of – perhaps parsley, basil, chervil or tarragon in the spring or summer, sage or rosemary in the winter months.

The softer herbs may be simply used as whole leaves, but the harder herbs (such as rosemary, sage or thyme) will need to be picked from the stem first and then chopped finely to make them palatable (see page 25). Imagine trying to chew on a raw rosemary sprig and then on a piece of parsley – the former is difficult and unpleasant, the latter easy and delicious.

In the spring, leaves of wild garlic are a beautiful addition to this dish. Simply wash them carefully, then spread one or 2 across the breast under the skin, one at a time, then fold the skin over to encase the leaves.

The summer is a perfect time to eat lots of raw, crisp and fresh salads that refresh not only the taste buds but also the spirits. I use less cream and butter in the summer, favouring olive oil dressings for dishes instead or the acidity of citrus or fruit juices, sour cream, yogurt or crème fraîche to lift flavours.

This recipe could easily be adapted by using a variety of different vegetables, depending on what looks good in the shop or on the market stall. Equally interchangeable are the grains. Try using spelt, barley or pasta instead, such as orzo, conchiglie, farfalle or orecchiette. Simply cook the pasta in the normal way in boiling salted water, drain and toss in olive oil to prevent it from sticking together, then fold into the vegetables and herbs.

It is advisable to prepare the salad before cooking the chicken so that it has time to marinate. »

SERVES 4

FOR THE SALAD
150g wild rice, or another grain, pasta or pulse of your choice
2 firm courgettes
2 sticks celery
½ bulb fennel
A few leaves summer cabbage

FOR THE DRESSING
4tbsp olive oil
1tbsp mixed chopped herbs, as chosen for the chicken
1 lemon or lime, juice

4 boneless free-range or organic chicken breasts, skin on
A few sprigs herbs of your choice (see intro)
Olive oil, for drizzling
150g mayonnaise (see page 79) or sour cream, to serve
Lemon wedges, to serve

Bring the wild rice to the boil in a saucepan of salted water and then turn the heat down to a simmer. Cook until just done, approximately 20–30 minutes. It is advisable to taste a grain or two frequently while the rice is cooking, as you do not want the grains to overcook or burst – instead they should retain a little firmness to the bite. (Take care, as other grains or pasta may take less time to cook – follow the instructions on the packet.)

Meanwhile, grate the courgettes on the largest side of a cheese grater and place in a large bowl. Slice the celery and fennel as finely as possible with a sharp knife and add to the courgettes. Remove the thick central veins of the cabbage leaves, then roll the leaves together like a cigar. Shred across as thinly as possible, and add to the salad. Leave covered in a cool place.

Place the dressing ingredients in a separate bowl, season with some sea salt and freshly ground pepper and mix with a fork or whisk until well amalgamated.

Drain the rice well and, while still warm, toss with the dressing and leave on one side. »

232

Lay the chicken breasts on a chopping board and carefully lift the skin away on one edge lengthwise. Fill the cavities with a few of the herbs (whole or chopped, see intro) and then fold the skin back over to its original position, encasing the herbs neatly. Season the breasts all over with sea salt and freshly ground pepper and drizzle with a little olive oil.

Heat a shallow, heavy-based, lidded frying pan with a dash of olive oil and, once hot, place the chicken breasts in, skin-side down. Cook over a medium to high heat until the skin is crisp and dark golden in colour. Turn the breasts over and cook in the same way until golden.

Add a splash of water, then place a lid on the pan, turn the heat down to low and continue to cook the chicken until done (approximately 5–6 minutes further). Test the doneness by inserting a skewer or small knife into the meat. If the juices run clear (not pink) the chicken is ready. Remove the pan from the heat and allow to cool, covered, while the grain salad is assembled.

Taste the wild rice for seasoning and then stir gently but thoroughly into the prepared vegetables, making sure all the ingredients are lightly coated in the dressing. Adjust the seasoning if necessary. Scatter the salad onto a serving dish.

Place the chicken breasts on top of the salad or, if you wish, using a sharp knife slice each chicken breast into 3 or 4 on the angle and arrange over and around the salad. This allows the beautiful layers of herbs within to be more visible.

Finally, drizzle over the chicken juices from the pan and serve with a pot of mayonnaise or a dollop of sour cream and lemon wedges.

This salad is equally lovely served with poached fillets of salmon perhaps, a selection of soft cheeses or cold roasted meats.

Baked fillet of plaice with chervil & spring onion

When I was growing up, my mother used to say that she disliked cooking fish at home as she felt it made the house smell. I fear that it stemmed more from a problem with the level of freshness of the fish that was available to us at the time. Living inland, as we did, meant that a reliable supply of freshly caught fish was a rarity.

Even now, I do not believe that 'smackingly' fresh fish is easily found up and down the land, unless one lives close to the coast or has a productive river or lake nearby. Most supermarkets have fish counters, but their displays often look to me as if the fish have recently been defrosted from frozen, are dripping with water, and do not look tempting in any way.

Getting to know a local fishmonger, how busy they are, and therefore how often their stock is turned over, would give good guidance as to which fish to buy and which to avoid. However, it would be preferable to not serve fish on your menu at all, if the freshness is questionable.

SERVES 2

50g butter, plus extra for the potatoes and asparagus

2 fillets plaice or another fish of your choice (180g total) – try hake, cod, lemon sole, halibut or brill

1tbsp finely sliced spring onion

2tsp chopped chervil (or dill, if unavailable)

½ lemon, finely grated zest

500g even-sized new potatoes

1 bunch green asparagus (approximately 12 spears)

Green mayonnaise (see page 79), to serve (optional)

Take 2 sheets of aluminium foil or parchment paper approximately A4 size and lay them side by side on the chopping board. Spread a quarter of the butter, slightly off centre, down the middle of each one, and place each fish fillet on top of the butter. Season generously with sea salt and freshly ground pepper, scatter the spring onion and herbs over and then the lemon zest.

Place the remaining butter on the top of the fillets, then fold the foil or parchment over and seal around the edges of the packages firmly, making them watertight envelopes. This is best done by crimping, in other words folding and pressing the pleats as you go. It is important that the juices cannot escape when the fillets are in the oven. These may be left in the fridge for a few hours before baking.

Scrub the potatoes well, pulling away any loose skins, and leave in a small saucepan of salted water. Wash the asparagus and trim away the tough base of the stalks.

Heat the oven to 180°C/fan oven 160°C/mark 4. Place the fish packages on a baking sheet and bake for 15–20 minutes, assuming the fillets are 1–1.5cm thick. (Cook for a little longer if thicker.) To check the doneness, remove the tray from the oven and open one corner of a package carefully. With a small knife, pierce the fillet – it should flake apart easily. If it still shows some resistance to the knife, reseal the package and continue to cook for a few more minutes.

Meanwhile, simmer the potatoes until almost tender, approximately 7–12 minutes depending on the size. Drain, season with salt and pepper, add a small slice of butter, cover and leave them in the pan. As they steam gently in the latent heat, they will continue to cook, flavoured by the butter.

Meanwhile, cook the asparagus in a little boiling salted water for 1–2 minutes (they hardly need any cooking), drain and then keep them in the pan, season with salt and pepper and a little slice of butter.

To serve, place a package on each plate and very slightly open each to reveal the fish inside. Serve immediately with the warm potatoes and asparagus alongside. The juices in the package will serve as the sauce. Alternatively, you could serve this dish with green mayonnaise.

Pavlova meringue with strawberries & spring rhubarb

SERVES 4–6–8 DEPENDING ON APPETITE
4 medium stalks rhubarb
1 orange, juice
½tbsp caster sugar
400g strawberries

TO SERVE
1 brown sugar pavlova or individual meringues (see page 131)
Double cream, stiffly whipped, or vanilla ice cream
Mint sprigs or leaves

Trim the leaf end and base end away from the rhubarb stalks and wash. Cut slightly on the angle into 2cm lengths and place in a wide-based medium pan, ideally in one layer. Add orange juice and sugar and cover with a lid. Bring slowly to a simmer and cook until barely soft, approximately 2–3 minutes. Check often, as the rhubarb cooks surprisingly quickly. Remove from the heat and allow to cool down in the pan, covered.

Meanwhile, prepare the strawberries. Remove the green leaves and slice each one into 2 or 3 depending on the size and place in a serving bowl. Carefully pour the cooled rhubarb over including the juices. Do not mix the fruit together at this stage, as the rhubarb is very delicate. Leave for up to 1 hour in the fridge to macerate.

To serve, gently spoon the whipped cream or vanilla ice cream into the pavlova or dollop it carefully onto the individual meringues. Carefully arrange the fruits (without the juices) over and around, making sure that the shapes and colours are distributed evenly. Decorate with sprigs of mint. Serve the juices in a small jug to go alongside.

Cheddar, sweetcorn & basil soufflé

Despite the bad reputation soufflés seem to have regarding their temperamental behaviour, they are really relatively simple to assemble and cook – and can be a source of tremendous pride once the basics have been mastered. The base may be made up to 2 days in advance and then finished and baked just before eating, thus minimising the time required in the kitchen on the day.

SERVES 4

50g unsalted butter
50g plain flour
2 bay leaves
1 tsp Dijon mustard
300ml milk
150g grated cheese – ideally Cheddar, Lancashire, Cheshire or Comté

2 cobs sweetcorn
1tbsp chopped basil or another herb of your choice
4 large free-range or organic eggs
Olive oil, for greasing

In a medium saucepan, heat the butter until melted. Add the flour and stir over a low heat until the mixture starts to gently sizzle, but do not allow it to colour. Add sea salt and freshly ground pepper, then the bay leaves and mustard.

Pour in the milk slowly, stirring continually over the heat, making sure the liquid stays smooth throughout. A wooden spoon is best for this, but if lumps start to appear, use a whisk to break them up.

The sauce will thicken as it simmers and should, after a few minutes, become a smooth, white, shiny base for your soufflé. Remove from the heat, taste and add ¾ of the grated cheese, stirring until well amalgamated. Remove the bay leaves and discard.

If you wish, the base may now be cooled and covered with clingfilm. Left in the fridge, it will last for up to 3 days. »

Autumn and WINTER

When you are ready to cook the soufflé, remove the leaves and hairs from the sweetcorn, then lay the cobs flat on a chopping board. Cut along the length of the corn with a small sharp knife, removing the kernels. Put these into a small saucepan, then with the back of the knife scrape the remaining 'milk' from the husks and add to the corn, with salt and pepper and just enough water to cover the base of the pan.

Place the pan over a medium heat, cover with a lid and cook the sweetcorn kernels for 1–2 minutes or until almost tender. Add the chopped basil and mix well. Drain away any excess juices.

Heat the oven to 180°C/fan oven 160°C/mark 4. Wipe or brush the inside of a 15cm-diameter ovenproof bowl or dish with a little olive oil.

Separate the eggs and place the whites in a large clean bowl. Add the yolks to the cheese sauce, stirring well together. (If the sauce has been in the fridge for a day or two, it will have set solidly, so some vigorous stirring will be necessary to loosen it.)

Using an electric whisk or mixer, whisk the egg whites until very firm, and stir half of this into the cheese sauce until completely smooth. Alternatively, this may be done by hand, but this will take a little more time and effort. Then, very gently, stir in the remaining whites (a few lumps of whites within the mix will be fine). Pour half this mixture into the prepared dish. Scatter with the sweetcorn, then cover with the remaining soufflé mix.

Sprinkle with the remaining ¼ of the grated cheese and bake in the centre of the oven for 25–30 minutes or until puffed and golden on the outside. The inside should be mostly cooked, leaving the centre very slightly runny, as this will act as the sauce for your soufflé. You may like to check by pushing a knife or skewer into the centre after 20 minutes; if it has a lot of liquid sticking to it when you pull it away, it will need a few more minutes cooking. Serve immediately – with aplomb!

Brussels sprouts with pecans, lemon zest & butter

Everyone eats Brussels sprouts, but do they really like them? Too often one finds them either overcooked or undercooked (I am not sure which is worse), and worst of all, the poor things have often had their bases cut with a cross – in theory, to make the cooking more even, but to my eye, this destroys the look of them.

Here, the lovely Brussels sprouts are tended with care and attention, flavoured with a kick of lemon zest and the added texture of toasted pecans. They are perfect served as an accompaniment to the Cheddar cheese soufflé (see previous page) and are also delicious with the braised pheasant (see page 247) for a more robust meal.

SERVES 4
400g Brussels sprouts (20–25 in number, depending on size)
20g unsalted butter
50g pecans, roughly sliced or chopped
1 lemon, grated zest

Wash and slice the sprouts roughly into 4 or 5. Bring a medium pan of salted water to the boil and cook the sprouts for 1–2 minutes or until al dente (still retaining some crunch). Drain well.

Meanwhile, in a separate pan or frying pan over a medium to high heat, melt the butter with the pecans. Fry for 1–2 minutes, stirring occasionally, until the nuts start to smell toasted, but take care as they will burn easily.

Add the drained sprouts to the pan and season well with salt, freshly ground pepper and lemon zest. Toss together over a high heat to warm everything together, taking care not to burn the delicate leaves, or the nuts, and serve as soon as possible, piping hot.

Comice pear, Comté, walnut & lemon salad

Choose a selection of salad leaves for this, such as watercress, treviso, romaine or frisée.

SERVES 4
A selection of salad leaves, approximately 200g
Olive oil
2 medium ripe pears, washed
100g Comté cheese
1 small lemon, cut into 6 wedges, pips removed
A handful walnuts, roughly chopped

Pick through the salad leaves, discarding any discoloured leaves or long stalks. Wash the leaves in cold water, drain well and dry carefully in a salad spinner. These leaves will stay deliciously crisp, stored in an air-tight container, in the salad drawer of the fridge for up to 3 days.

To serve, place a handful of salad leaves per person into a large bowl. Drizzle with olive oil, salt and freshly ground pepper, toss gently by hand and arrange on the individual plates, making sure that each plate has a variety of colours and shapes.

Using a vegetable peeler, peel the pears (including the skin) over the salad in long ribbons, letting them drop over and around the leaves. Alternatively, slice them finely. Next, shave the cheese in the same way over the salad.

Last of all, squeeze the lemon segments over and around, followed by a final drizzle of olive oil and a sprinkling of chopped walnuts.

Braised pheasant with soft Parmesan polenta, chestnuts & raisins

A brace of pheasant used to be one of the less expensive options on the market in the autumn and winter months. Sadly, the costs have risen in recent years unless, of course, you are lucky enough to know of a local farmer who may sell them at the gate – go and ask. (You will, of course, have to cope with the plucking and drawing, as the birds will not be 'oven ready' if you buy them in this way.) Use a chicken or duck if pheasant is not available.

SERVES 3–5 DEPENDING ON APPETITES

FOR THE BRAISED PHEASANT
1 pheasant, oven ready
2tbsp olive oil
75g unsalted butter
1 large onion, peeled and chopped into 8–10 wedges
1 large carrot, peeled and thickly sliced
1 celery stick, thickly sliced
1 large sprig each rosemary, bay and thyme
1 large glass red wine
1 large orange, peel and juice
500ml chicken or vegetable stock, plus a little extra if required
1tbsp raisins
6–8 chestnuts (vacuum-packed are fine), cut in half
A few parsley leaves or celery leaves, roughly chopped

FOR THE POLENTA
500ml milk
500ml water
1tsp finely chopped fresh rosemary, thyme or sage
1 clove garlic, peeled and crushed
200g polenta
100g unsalted butter
75g grated Parmesan cheese, plus 25g for finishing the dish

Try to remove the visible shot (if any) from the pheasant, either by hand or with a small knife. Wipe the inside of the bird with kitchen paper and remove the legs, first by cutting through the skin at the side of the breast, then pulling the leg outwards, which will break the ball and socket joint by the backbone. This will leave the breasts attached to the crown.

Using a sharp heavy knife or heavy scissors, cut the backbone away from the carcass down each side. Season all the pieces well – the legs, the crown with the breasts attached, and the backbone. Heat the oven to 165 °C/fan oven 145°C/mark 3.

Heat half the olive oil and half the butter in a heavy, deep frying pan and seal the pieces of pheasant until golden brown on all sides. This may take 5–7 minutes. You are not cooking the meat here, simply browning the outsides, so it is important that you keep turning over the pieces in the hot fat. Use tongs to protect your fingers from the spitting oil.

Remove the pieces of pheasant to a large ovenproof dish. Add the remaining oil and butter to the pan, followed by the vegetables, and fry over a medium to high heat until they start to colour, approximately 3–4 minutes. Season generously with sea salt and freshly ground pepper, add the herbs and then the wine, orange juice, peel and stock. Bring to a rapid boil, then pour everything over the pheasant pieces.

Shake the dish gently to settle the contents and to level the vegetables covering the meat. Cover with a lid or a tightly fitting piece of aluminium foil, and braise in the oven for up to 1 hour. Halfway through the cooking time, lift the lid and and turn the pieces of pheasant over to ensure even cooking. If the juices have started to evaporate and the meat looks a little dry, top up with extra warm stock or water from a kettle.

Test the doneness by piercing a leg with a small knife or skewer. If the meat feels tender, and slightly falls away from the bone, it is ready. Remove from the oven and allow to cool in the dish.

When cool enough to handle, lift the pieces of pheasant from the liquid onto a large plate and carefully remove the meat from the bones, shredding it a little with a fork or your fingers into a small pan. Discard the bones and skin and strain the juices over the meat, skimming away any fat that rises to the surface.

Taste for seasoning, then add the raisins and chestnuts to the pan. Leave on one side in a cool place while you cook the polenta.

Gently heat the milk with the water, herbs, garlic and some salt and pepper. Once the mixture has almost come to the simmer, slowly pour in the polenta, stirring or whisking continuously. When all the polenta has been added, turn up the heat a little. The polenta will be liquid to start, but as it cooks, it will thicken, so keep stirring or whisking. After 5–10 minutes, the polenta will look like a thick yellow porridge. Taste it and if it is at all grainy, continue to stir over a medium heat until cooked. Remove from the heat and stir in the butter and the 75g Parmesan. Taste and adjust the seasoning if necessary. Cover and keep warm.

Bring the pheasant up to the simmer for a few minutes until thoroughly reheated. Do not overcook, or else the meat will become stringy.

To serve, divide the soft polenta among the warm plates and sprinkle with the remaining Parmesan. Spoon the pheasant including the juices over the top or on one side, and scatter with the chopped parsley or celery leaves. Serve immediately.

The Festive Season

Sometimes one simply needs a little hit of sweetness
and there seems to be no rhyme or reason as to when this craving
will arise. Being a treat means perhaps there is no need
for an excuse or a reason – it is simply needed. It could be after dinner
when perhaps a dessert has not been served, with coffee or a fresh
mint or ginger tisane (see page 262), or after a light lunch
when one more mouthful is craved. Or perhaps mid-afternoon,
when energy levels and spirits are down, one little mouthful
of sugar is all that is required.

The giving of gifts is a big part of any festive season,
and while no one wishes to feel mean at this time, the costs can
escalate all too easily, especially at Christmas. Creating
one's own gifts is one way of not only trimming the expense,
but also giving something that is unique. So make more sweetmeats
than you need, and give away some of your handiwork,
wrapped in tissue paper and tied with ribbon or raffia
and a beautiful gift tag.

Sweetmeats

Homemade marzipan
Dates filled with marzipan
Orange zest and cinnamon shortbtread
Marzipan and mincemeat pasties
Dark chocolate with nuts and raisins

Fresh ginger and mint tisane

Homemade marzipan

Following this recipe are a couple for marzipan sweetmeats, so make this marzipan first. The recipe makes enough for both items, approximately 16 mincemeat pasties and 12 filled dates. The marzipan will keep in the fridge for up to a week.

250g ground almonds
250g icing sugar, plus a little extra if needed
1 large or 2 small egg whites
1½tsp lemon juice
1 drop bitter almond essence

In a food processor, mix the almonds and sugar together for 1–2 minutes until well blended. Add the remaining ingredients until a dry-ish ball is formed. Alternatively, mix all together in a bowl by hand.

Knead the marzipan gently together until it forms a smooth ball, adding a drop or two of water if it seems too dry or a little icing sugar if it seems too wet. Wrap and chill for a few hours.

Dates filled with marzipan

Dates, almonds and pistachio nuts – a wonderfully evocative combination of tastes and textures, which bring back memories to me of wandering aimlessly through markets in Istanbul and Marrakesh over the years.

However, perhaps my first taste of the 'exotic' was as a very young child. Often on a Sunday afternoon, my father would take himself off to the kitchen, don an apron, and set to work making Turkish Delight for us all. For some reason it was the only recipe he could cook, and it would take him seemingly hours and hours to make just a handful! While we listened to the sounds of clanging pots and pans and smelled the fragrant aromas of rose water and sugar through the crack in the door, we patiently waited for the dish of treasure to emerge, along with his enormously proud smile.

MAKES 12
¼ of the marzipan recipe (see page 252)
Icing sugar, to dust
12 medjool dates
1tbsp pistachio nuts, very finely chopped

Make an incision down the length of one side of each date and remove the stone.

Roll the marzipan into a sausage shape approximately ½cm thick, using a dusting of icing sugar if it becomes sticky. Cut into 12 equal lengths.

Fill each of the dates with a piece of marzipan. Lay them in a row, marzipan filling upwards. Using a clean finger 'brush' the top of the marzipan with a little water or some of the remaining egg white from the marzipan, then, with dry fingers, sprinkle with the chopped pistachio nuts and leave on a small plate until ready to serve.

Marzipan & mincemeat pasties

MAKES 16

Approximately ¾ of the marzipan recipe (see page 252)
200g mincemeat (Clarke's is best!)
Icing sugar, for rolling and dusting
Vanilla ice cream, to serve

Divide the marzipan into 2 evenly sized balls and roll one of them out like pastry, to approximately ½cm thick, using icing sugar instead of flour to prevent sticking. If it is difficult to handle, do not worry, simply gather the pieces up together, and start rolling again.

Cut the rolled-out marzipan into 8 x 8cm discs. Repeat with the second half. Heat the oven to 180°C/fan oven 160°C/mark 4.

Place ½tsp mincemeat in the centre of each marzipan disc. With your finger, brush the rim of each disc with cold water.

Gather the edges of the marzipan up into a Cornish pasty shape, pressing the marzipan over the mincemeat and gently pressing the edges together and crimping them decoratively. Place onto a baking sheet lined with silicone wax paper or baking paper.

Using a tea strainer or small sieve, dust a little extra icing sugar over the pasties and bake for 8–10 minutes or until golden.

Serve either warm or at room temperature, dusted again with icing sugar, with a scoop of ice cream and ideally a glass of Madeira, port or Champagne.

Orange zest & cinnamon shortbread

The dough for these biscuits, once shaped and coated in cinnamon sugar, freezes well – and needs only a few minutes' defrosting before slicing and baking.

MAKES APPROXIMATELY 20 BISCUITS
300g plain flour, plus extra for
  dusting
½tsp ground cinnamon, plus
  extra for coating
200g cold unsalted butter, cubed
Pinch sea salt
100g granulated sugar
1 large orange, finely grated zest
20g demerara sugar

Put the flour, cinnamon and butter in a large bowl with the salt and, using your fingertips, rub the butter into the flour. This action is simple enough and involves the ingredients being rubbed together with the fingertips, little by little, and lifted up each time, allowing the flour to fall back into the bowl. This keeps the mixture light and airy.

Once the flour mixture resembles fine breadcrumbs, stir in the sugar and orange zest, spreading them evenly throughout. Using your hands, push the mixture firmly together, kneading gently into a smooth dough and then into a thick, even sausage shape, using a light dusting of flour if it becomes sticky. If on the other hand it seems too dry to form a ball, sprinkle it with a little cold water and push gently together until smooth.

Mix the demerara with a good pinch of cinnamon, scatter onto a large plate and roll the sausage in this so that it is coated. Wrap tightly in clingfilm and leave in the fridge for at least 1 hour before cutting.

Heat the oven to 150°C/fan oven 130°C/mark 2 and line a baking sheet with a piece of silicone wax paper. With a sharp knife, cut the chilled dough into ½cm discs. Lay on the paper, spacing them well apart.

Bake for 20–25 minutes or until a very pale golden. Depending on your oven, the tray may need turning around halfway through to achieve an even bake. Allow the biscuits to cool, then eat soon after or remove to an airtight container where they will last nicely for up to 1 week.

Dark chocolate with nuts & raisins

This is a perfect 'sweet hit' to serve at the end of a meal or to nibble mid-afternoon.

SERVES 4
200g good-quality dark chocolate, ideally 70–80 per cent cocoa solids
75g mixed nuts, such as almonds, pistachios, hazelnuts and pecans
75g raisins, sultanas or currants
Sea salt (optional)

Chop the chocolate and place in a medium bowl. Place a small pan containing a small amount of water over a low heat and sit the bowl over the top. The water must not come in contact with the bowl, rather the gentle steam will be all that is needed to melt the chocolate.

Allow the chocolate to sit over the heat for a few minutes, without stirring, until it is completely liquid. Remember that chocolate melts in your hand, so excess heat is not required here.

Meanwhile, line a 20cm square baking sheet with a piece of parchment paper or silicone wax paper, then prepare the nuts and fruits, roughly chopping or breaking the nuts, separating the fruits if they have stuck to one another, and mixing them together.

Give the chocolate a quick stir and pour it on to the paper allowing it to spread by itself, but helping it a little by gently tapping the baking sheet as it levels. The chocolate will not cover the sheet entirely.

Working quickly, before the chocolate sets, sprinkle over the chopped nuts and fruits. Tap the sheet gently again to encourage the fruits and nuts to sink into the chocolate, but not be covered by it. Sprinkle with a very little sea salt, if you like.

Allow the chocolate to cool, then chill in the fridge before breaking or cutting it into rough shards and serving. If kept cool, it will last for up to 5 days, but as with most things – the fresher the better.

Fresh ginger & mint tisane

I love coffee, and I cannot imagine starting my day without the
ritual of grinding the beans, measuring the grounds, boiling
the kettle, stirring the hot water into the coffee just so, not too
vigorously, not too gently, allowing it to settle for a minute or two,
then pouring it through a strainer into a cup (definitely not a mug
for me). Adding hardly any sugar at all (no one is to know) with
one stir, then pouring the very light cream into the top, watching
it swirl as it blends slowly into the darkness, until the balance of
cream and coffee is just so – then taking a deep breath in…

However, as much as I love coffee, there is no beating a hot,
steaming cup of fresh ginger and mint after a meal, especially at
night. It not only aids digestion but also sleep. Any mint variety is
fine, but the best is spearmint, which has pointed, slightly jagged
reddish-green leaves. And at the first inkling of a cold, a sore throat
or an ache or pain, I find that fresh ginger cures most ailments.
Singers swear by it, as it clears the nasal passages and the throat. Or
you can serve this simply as a calming, soothing, delicious way to
end your day.

Writing this reminds me of my mentor Alice Waters and her
restaurant (my favourite in the world) Chez Panisse in Berkeley,
California. After each meal a glass pot of steaming tisane (lemon
verbena, mint or lemon thyme perhaps, depending on the time of
year) is poured at the table into beautiful thick glass tumblers,
which are etched with the distinctive 'Chez Panisse' script.

SERVES 2
A piece of fresh ginger, roughly the size of 3 walnuts
3 or 4 sprigs mint, including the stems

Boil a kettle and warm a medium sized tea pot with a little boiling water.

Wash the ginger, peel and trim away any discoloured edges. Slice as finely as possible with a very sharp knife – a blunt knife will bruise the root and spill the precious juices over the chopping board. Wash the mint gently, without crushing the leaves.

Tip away the warming water in the pot, then place the ginger slices in with the mint sprigs.

Boil the kettle again and pour the hot water into the pot until ¾ full. Place the lid on the top and allow to infuse for 2–3 minutes. Pour into cups, mugs or thick glasses and allow to cool a little before tasting and enjoying.

Afterwards, the pot may be refilled as before, often resulting in an even stronger brew than the first. A tip – do not throw away the ginger and mint, as they may be used one more time the morning after.

Index

The main recipe titles in the index are marked with a *, **, *** denoting a recipe's simplicity (or relative complexity) to prepare and cook.

A

A lovely ham & vegetable broth* 100
Apple Brown Betty** 205
apples
  Bircher muesli with nuts & apple 49
  Bramley apples filled with cinnamon, brown sugar, pecans & sultanas 164
  Rhubarb and Bramley apple muffins 128
Apricot & vanilla jam*** 43
asparagus
  Scrambled eggs with spring onion & asparagus 85
avocados
  Hamburgers with guacamole, tomato & cucumber salad 101
Avocado on toasted sour dough with egg & smoked paprika** 63

B

bacon
  Sausages, bacon, mushrooms & eggs 69
  'Baked beans' with vegetables & herbs 220
Baked cheese in a box* 148
Baked eggs, mushrooms & spinach** 70
Baked fillet of plaice with chervil & spring onion** 235
Baked onion soup with Gruyère toasts** 156
Baked toasts for scooping or spreading* 192
Banana, chocolate, pecan & cinnamon loaf* 141
berries
  Yogurt, blueberry & strawberry smoothie 34
Braised duck legs in orange & rosemary with celeriac mash** 223

Braised neck of lamb with spices, orange, rosemary & lentils** 110
Braised pheasant with soft Parmesan polenta, chestnuts & raisins*** 247
Bramley apples filled with cinnamon, brown sugar, pecans & sultanas* 164
breadcrumbs 152
breads
  Seeded granary bread 39
  Soda bread with cheese, pickles & celery 77
Brown sugar meringues** 131
Brussels sprouts
  Chicory, grape & Brussels sprout salad with hazelnuts 108
Brussels sprouts with pecans, lemon zest & butter** 243

C

cabbage
  Winter slaw with red cabbage, parsnip & pomegranate 114
carrots
  Chilled carrot soup with yogurt, coriander & cumin wafer toasts 228
cauliflower
  Winter green salad with cauliflower, almonds, currants & mustard 178
celeriac
  Braised duck legs in orange & rosemary with celeriac mash 223
chard
  Spiced chard leaves 225
Cheddar, anchovy & rosemary scones with black pepper* 135
Cheddar, sweetcorn & basil soufflé** 240
cheese
  Baked cheese in a box 148
  Baked onion soup with Gruyère toasts 156
  Braised pheasant with soft Parmesan polenta, chestnuts & raisins 247
  Mushrooms on toast with chives & Swiss cheese 132

Open omelette with fresh goat's cheese & herbs 64
Polentina soup with Parmesan 195
Pumpkin, blue cheese & walnut galette 86
Rabbit with pappardelle, parsley & Parmesan 182
Roasted chicken & mozzarella open sandwiches with basil 74
Savoury bread & butter pudding with cheese & herbs 155
Soda bread with cheese, pickles & celery 77
Tomato, mozzarella & basil galette 180
Whipped cream cheese 192
chicken
  Chicken liver & honey pâté 200
  Herb-filled chicken breasts with wild rice salad & citrus dressing 231
  Light chicken stock 176
  Roasted chicken & mozzarella open sandwiches with basil 74
  Roasted chicken with potatoes, carrots, red onion & watercress 172
Chicken liver & honey pâté*** 200
chickpeas
  Soup of tomato, curly kale & chickpeas 188
  Warm chickpeas with spinach 215
Chicory, grape & Brussels sprout salad with hazelnuts* 108
Chilled carrot soup with yogurt, coriander & cumin wafer toasts* 228
chocolate
  Banana, chocolate, pecan & cinnamon loaf 141
  Dark chocolate with nuts & raisins 260
  Hot mocha drink with whipped cream 53
Chopped salad** 203
chopping 26
citrus fruit
  Fresh lemonade 122

Herb-filled chicken breasts
with wild rice salad & citrus
dressing 231
Mixed winter juices 46
Pink grapefruit & blood orange
segments 32
Winter fruit salad 46
Cod & smoked haddock pie
with leeks, mushrooms, parsley
& potato** 159
coffee
Hot mocha drink with whipped
cream 53
Cold poached ham with raw
vegetables & mayonnaise** 98
Comice pear, Comté, walnut
& lemon salad* 244
cookies
Oatmeal, sultana &
maple syrup cookies 125
cracked wheat
Vine tomato, parsley &
cracked wheat salad 89
cucumber
Hamburgers with guacamole,
tomato & cucumber
salad 101
Spiced lamb koftas with yogurt,
mint & cucumber 211
curly kale
Soup of tomato, curly kale &
chickpeas 188

D

Dark chocolate with nuts &
raisins** 260
Dates filled with marzipan** 255
dicing 22
dried fruits
Dark chocolate with nuts
& raisins 260
Dates filled with marzipan 255
Granola with oats, apricot,
dates & almonds 37
Oatmeal, sultana & maple
syrup cookies 125
drinks
Fresh ginger & mint
tisane 262
Fresh lemonade 122
Hot mocha drink with whipped
cream 53
Mixed winter juices 46
Yogurt, blueberry &
strawberry smoothie 34
duck
Braised duck legs in orange &
rosemary with celeriac
mash 223

E

Egg mayonnaise with
anchovy soldiers** 126
eggs
Avocado on toasted sour
dough with egg & smoked
paprika 63
Baked eggs, mushrooms &
spinach 70
Kedgeree 56
Open omelette with fresh
goat's cheese &
herbs 64
Sausages, bacon, mushrooms
& eggs 69
Scrambled eggs with spring
onion & asparagus 85
equipment 18

F

fennel
Fish soup with rice &
fennel 146
fish
Baked fillet of plaice with
chervil & spring onion 235
Cod & smoked haddock pie
with leeks, mushrooms, parsley
& potato 159
Egg mayonnaise with anchovy
soldiers 126
Kedgeree 56
Marinated fresh anchovies 104
Potato pancake with smoked
salmon & sour
cream 66
Tuna sandwich with radish &
cucumber 79
Fish cakes*** 151
Fish soup with rice &
fennel** 146
Fish thumbs* 136
food safety 28
Fresh ginger & mint tisane* 262
Fresh lemonade* 122
frittata
Pea, mint & potato frittata with
a salad of herbs 208

G

galette
Pumpkin, blue cheese & walnut
galette 86
Tomato, mozzarella & basil
galette 180
garlic
crushing 25
Granola with oats, apricot, dates
& almonds* 37

H

ham
A lovely ham & vegetable
broth 100
Cold poached ham with raw
vegetables & mayonnaise 98
Hamburgers with guacamole,
tomato & cucumber
salad** 101
Herbed & spiced meatballs* 185
Herb-filled chicken breasts with
wild rice salad & citrus
dressing** 231
herbs
Baked fillet of plaice with
chervil & spring onion 235
Cheddar, anchovy & rosemary
scones with black pepper 135
Cheddar, sweetcorn & basil
soufflé 240
Chilled carrot soup with yogurt,
coriander & cumin wafer
toasts 228
chives 26
chopping 25, 26
Fresh ginger & mint tisane 262
Mushrooms on toast with chives
& Swiss cheese 132
Open omelette with fresh goat's
cheese & herbs 64
Pasta with summer vegetables,
basil & pine nuts 196
Pea, mint & potato frittata with
a salad of herbs 208
Rabbit with pappardelle, parsley
& Parmesan 182
Roasted chicken & mozzarella
open sandwiches with basil 74
Savoury bread & butter pudding
with cheese & herbs 155
Spiced lamb koftas with yogurt,
mint & cucumber 211
Steamed mussels with cream,
parsley & spring onions 163
Tomato, mozzarella & basil
galette 180
Vine tomato, parsley & cracked
wheat salad 89
Homemade marzipan* 252
Hot mocha drink with whipped
cream* 53

I

ice cream
Strawberry ripple ice cream 216

J

jam
Apricot & vanilla jam 43

K

Kedgeree*** 56
kitchen rules 17
koftas
  Spiced lamb koftas with yogurt, mint & cucumber 211

L

lamb
  Braised neck of lamb with spices, orange, rosemary & lentils 110
  Spiced lamb koftas with yogurt, mint & cucumber 211
Leek & pea soup* 168
leeks
  Cod & smoked haddock pie with leeks, mushrooms, parsley & potato 159
  Savoury tart filled with leek & field mushrooms 117
lentils
  Braised neck of lamb with spices, orange, rosemary & lentils 110
Light chicken stock* 176

M

Marinated fresh anchovies* 104
marzipan
  Dates filled with marzipan 255
  Homemade marzipan 252
Marzipan & mincemeat pasties** 258
mayonnaise 79, 82
  Cold poached ham with raw vegetables & mayonnaise 98
  Egg mayonnaise with anchovy soldiers 126
meatballs
  Herbed & spiced meatballs 185
menu planning 19
meringues
  Brown sugar meringues 131
mincemeat
  Marzipan & mincemeat pasties 258
Mixed winter juices* 46
muffins
  Rhubarb and Bramley apple muffins 128
mushrooms
  Baked eggs, mushrooms & spinach 70
  Cod & smoked haddock pie with leeks, mushrooms, parsley & potato 159
  Sausages, bacon, mushrooms & eggs 69
  Savoury tart filled with leek & field mushrooms 117
  Mushrooms on toast with chives & Swiss cheese** 132
mussels
  Steamed mussels with cream, parsley & spring onions 163

N

nuts and seeds
  Bircher muesli with nuts & apple 49
  Brussels sprouts with pecans, lemon zest & butter 243
  Chicory, grape & Brussels sprout salad with hazelnuts 108
  Comice pear, Comté, walnut & lemon salad 244
  Dark chocolate with nuts & raisins 260
  Granola with oats, apricot, dates & almonds 37
  Pain perdu with pecans 218
  Pasta with summer vegetables, basil & pine nuts 196
  Pumpkin, blue cheese & walnut galette 86
  Seeded granary bread 39
  Winter green salad with cauliflower, almonds, currants & mustard 178

O

Oatmeal, sultana & maple syrup cookies* 125
oats
  Bircher muesli with nuts & apple 49
  Granola with oats, apricot, dates & almonds 37
  Warm porridge with brown sugar 50
onions 22
  Baked onion soup with Gruyère toasts 156
  dicing 22
  Pissaladière 92
Open omelette with fresh goat's cheese & herbs** 64
Orange zest & cinnamon shortbread** 259

P

Pain perdu with pecans* 218
pancakes
  Potato pancake with smoked salmon & sour cream 66
  Warm ricotta pancakes with maple syrup 59
pasta
  Rabbit with pappardelle, parsley & Parmesan 182
Pasta with summer vegetables, basil & pine nuts** 196
pastry
  Pissaladière 92
  Pumpkin, blue cheese & walnut galette 86
  Savoury tart filled with leek & field mushrooms 117
pâté
  Chicken liver & honey pâté 200
Pavlova meringue with strawberries & spring rhubarb*** 239
Pea & celery risotto with pea leaves** 107
Pea, mint & potato frittata with a salad of herbs*** 208
peas
  Leek & pea soup 168
pheasant
  Braised pheasant with soft Parmesan polenta, chestnuts & raisins 247
pies
  Cod & smoked haddock pie with leeks, mushrooms, parsley & potato 159
Pink grapefruit & blood orange segments** 32
Pissaladière* 92
polenta
  Braised pheasant with soft Parmesan polenta, chestnuts & raisins 247
Polentina soup with Parmesan* 195
potato
  Cod & smoked haddock pie with leeks, mushrooms, parsley & potato 159
  Pea, mint & potato frittata with a salad of herbs 208
  Roasted chicken with potatoes, carrots, red onion & watercress 172
Potato pancake with smoked salmon & sour cream*** 66
Pumpkin, blue cheese & walnut galette*** 86

R

Rabbit with pappardelle, parsley & Parmesan*** 182

Rhubarb and Bramley apple
  muffins* 128
rice
  Fish soup with rice &
    fennel 146
  Herb-filled chicken breasts with
    wild rice salad & citrus
      dressing 231
  Kedgeree 56
risotto** 177
  Pea & celery risotto with
    pea leaves 107
Roasted chicken & mozzarella
  open sandwiches with basil* 74
Roasted chicken with potatoes,
  carrots, red onion &
    watercress** 172

S
salads
  Chicory, grape & Brussels sprout
    salad with hazelnuts 108
  Chopped salad 203
  Comice pear, Comté, walnut &
    lemon salad 244
  Hamburgers with guacamole,
    tomato & cucumber salad 101
  Herb-filled chicken breasts with
    wild rice salad & citrus
      dressing 231
  Vine tomato, parsley & cracked
    wheat salad 89
  Winter fruit salad 46
  Winter green salad with
    cauliflower, almonds, currants
      & mustard 178
  Winter slaw with red cabbage,
    parsnip & pomegranate 114
salmon
  Potato pancake with smoked
    salmon & sour cream 66
sandwiches
  Roasted chicken & mozzarella
    open sandwiches with basil 74
  Tuna sandwich with radish &
    cucumber 79
Sausages, bacon, mushrooms
  & eggs** 69
Savoury bread & butter pudding
  with cheese & herbs* 155
Savoury tart filled with leek
  & field mushrooms*** 117
scones
  Cheddar, anchovy & rosemary
    scones with black pepper 135
Scrambled eggs with spring
  onion & asparagus** 85
Seeded granary bread** 39
settle a chopping board 22

shortbread
  Orange zest & cinnamon
    shortbread 259
slicing 23, 26
Soda bread with cheese, pickles
  & celery* 77
soufflé
  Cheddar, sweetcorn & basil
    soufflé 240
Soup of tomato, curly kale
  & chickpeas** 188
soups
  A lovely ham & vegetable
    broth 100
  Baked onion soup with Gruyère
    toasts 156
  Chilled carrot soup with yogurt,
    coriander & cumin wafer
      toasts 228
  Fish soup with rice & fennel
    146
  Leek & pea soup 168
  Polentina soup with
    Parmesan 195
Spiced chard leaves* 225
Spiced lamb koftas with yogurt,
  mint & cucumber** 211
spinach
  Baked eggs, mushrooms &
    spinach 70
  Warm chickpeas with
    spinach 215
spring onions 26
  Baked fillet of plaice with
    chervil & spring
      onion 235
  Scrambled eggs with spring
    onion & asparagus 85
Steamed mussels with cream,
  parsley & spring onions* 163
stock
  Light chicken stock 176
storage 28
Strawberry ripple ice
  cream** 216
sweetmeats
  Dark chocolate with nuts
    & raisins 260
  Dates filled with marzipan 255
  Marzipan & mincemeat pasties
    258
  Orange zest & cinnamon
    shortbread 259

T
Tartare sauce 82
tea bread
  Banana, chocolate, pecan
    & cinnamon loaf 141

tisane
  Fresh ginger & mint tisane 262
toast
  Avocado on toasted sour dough
    with egg & smoked paprika 63
  Baked eggs, mushrooms &
    spinach 70
  Baked onion soup with
    Gruyère toasts 156
  Baked toasts for scooping
    or spreading 192
  Chilled carrot soup with yogurt,
    coriander & cumin wafer
      toasts 228
  Egg mayonnaise with anchovy
    soldiers 126
  Mushrooms on toast with chives
    & Swiss cheese 132
tomatoes
  blanching and peeling 24
  Hamburgers with guacamole,
    tomato & cucumber salad 101
  Soup of tomato, curly kale &
    chickpeas 188
  Vine tomato, parsley & cracked
    wheat salad 89
  Tomato, mozzarella & basil
    galette*** 180
  Tuna sandwich with radish &
    cucumber** 79

V
vegetables
  slicing 23
Vine tomato, parsley & cracked
  wheat salad* 89

W
Warm chickpeas with
  spinach* 215
Warm porridge with brown
  sugar* 50
Warm ricotta pancakes with
  maple syrup*** 59
washing up 21
Whipped cream cheese* 192
Winter fruit salad** 46
Winter green salad with
  cauliflower, almonds, currants
    & mustard* 178
Winter slaw with red cabbage,
  parsnip & pomegranate* 114

Y
Yogurt, blueberry & strawberry
  smoothie* 34

Acknowledgements

The past year has been like no other and has challenged everyone. The constantly changing goalposts and tier systems within the hospitality industry have been devastating to so many. Although this has been an unbelievably stressful year for us all at Clarke's, we were fortunate with other opportunities offered to us.

While the Restaurant doors remained closed, we were able to supply home deliveries from our kitchen, allowing some of our customers a little taste of Clarke's in their own homes. In addition, the bakery, production kitchen and shops have remained open throughout – feeding the neighbourhood and beyond. We continue to honour our role as 'essential shops'!

Throughout this, I have had the rare freedom of being able to return home at the drop of a hat to continue with my writing, editing and re-editing. This is something I could not have achieved without the dedication and hard work of the Managers who have led from the front and who, together with their teams, have kept the business afloat. My enormous thanks go out to, in no particular order, Paul, Michele, Athene, Manuel and Manuel, Gabriele, Nolwenn, Rigi, Edward and Georgia, Taddeo, Colin, Adrian, Russell, Nigel, Cedric, Mai, Piotr and Piotr.

And where would any of us be without our wonderfully loyal customers? Over more than 35 years, layers and layers of followers have been built upon, and many have become friends. Even though it goes against my 'home counties' upbringing, I am embarrassed to write that we now even address some using their first names!

Some of their children are now bringing THEIR children, and although those visiting from abroad have been few and far between this year, we nevertheless have kept in touch with many of them, keeping the Clarke's flame burning, ready for their return. So, thank you all, from those just around the corner who drop by every day for their coffee and daily bread to those who keep in touch from across the continents and the oceans. We know you will be back – whenever it is safe to do so.

It is a well-known fact that asking a busy person for help is often the best route to take, as they will always find the time. Here, I will try to list those many busy people who kindly offered to be part of the wind beneath my wings throughout this process.

Liz Payne, Clarke's past Head Chef from the mid-80s who, from her home in the Yorkshire Dales, agreed (again) to test the recipes.

The delightful quartet who prepared, cooked, styled and photographed the dishes for me – Rosie Ramsden, Rosie French, Tabitha Hawkins and Lizzie Mayson – and who proved to be a dream to work with. Focused yet fun, talented yet modest, and despite my being probably twice their average age, always made me feel welcome and part of the gang.

Patrick Budge for being a most patient and sympathetic designer, and for making the whole process such an enjoyable experience for me. (He even tried some of the recipes out on his family while working through the layouts). I state categorically that this is my third and final book, however, if I ever change my mind, Patrick and the 'delightful quartet' will be my five ports of call!

Kay Halsey and Sophie Devlin for guiding me in making sure that the recipes and prose flowed seamlessly and were grammatically correct. As did Colin Hall, another busy perfectionist, who kindly and willingly agreed to cast his eye over more than one early draft. Ditto Michael Hall, who also doubles as a great godfather to Samuel, and Toby Treves, for his sage advice.

To the fabulously wonderful Paul and Pauline Smith for creating the most perfect *First Put on Your Apron* apron for my book.

To John Morton Morris for giving us all endless amounts of encouragement, for his unconditional support and for his unmatched eye for detail.

And finally, to 'my' three graces – Blanche, Claire and Fanny – who so sweetly agreed to write a few words of affirmation for the cover. So kind.

Thank you to all.

Spring 2021